RIDE A RHINO

This edition, issued in 1960, is for members of The Companion Book Club, 8 Long Acre, London, W.C.99, from which address particulars of membership may be obtained. The book is issued by arrangement with the original publishers, W. H. Allen & Co. Ltd.

Also by
MICHAELA DENIS
★

LEOPARD IN MY LAP

"A blessed companion is a book"—JERROLD

RIDE A RHINO

★

MICHAELA DENIS

THE COMPANION BOOK CLUB
LONDON

Made and printed in Great Britain
for The Companion Book Club (Odhams Press Ltd.)
by Odhams (Watford) Limited
Watford, Herts
S.1160.W.Q.

CONTENTS

ILLUSTRATIONS

*Photographs by Armand and Michaela Denis,
except where otherwise indicated*

ILLUSTRATIONS IN COLOUR

ILLUSTRATIONS IN BLACK AND WHITE

6

CHAPTER ONE

HOME AT LAST

"Michaela," said Angèle, my sister-in-law, "perhaps, when your travels are over, you and Armand will come and settle in the Ardennes. You could find a lovely house in the forest."

She gazed speculatively at us both, and I hated having to answer her as I did. I loved Belgium, but——

"Dear Angèle," I said, "it is no use pretending. My heart is in Africa."

I glanced at Armand, expecting him to confirm what I had said, but he only gave a shrug. "By the time we stop our wanderings," he said, "Africa will probably have changed. The place of your dreams is never as you imagine it."

Yes, I knew there was some truth in what he said, and yet I found it almost impossible to imagine that we might end our days in any other part of the world.

"But tell me," said Angèle, "what *is* it about Africa you love so much?"

I was unable to answer her, for how could I have begun to describe the sights and sounds and smells of Africa which never fail to draw me back and hold me in their spell?

Of course there would be that drive from the airport when you arrived, which made you wonder if you were mad ever to have wished to return. Why, oh why, should travellers have to enter exciting cities through the back door, as happens at Nairobi—and many other

7

places as well? But the slums and factories would be forgotten when you glanced upwards, far above the tumult of the jostling crowds in the streets, and saw a flight of crested cranes, with necks outstretched, winging their way across the vivid blue vastness of the sky. Then there would be the unmistakable smell of the red dust, which was so nauseating to some, yet a heady perfume to others such as me. And how could you describe the warm thrill of being recognized by your African friends, who remembered you as one of their own, albeit an adopted one, and greeted you in their resonant, musical voices? And what mere words could convey the majesty of the mountains or the glory of the National Parks, where big game roamed in greater profusion than anywhere else in the world?

* * *

The plane circled and dropped as lightly as a feather on to the runway of Nairobi's new airport. The old familiar feeling of excitement surged up again—the feeling that I was dropping into welcoming arms. We were back in Africa!

The customs officer greeted us like old friends. He asked us if we had enjoyed our trip and enquired if we had brought any members of our family with us, by which he meant Minnie the mongoose or Bertram the bushbaby. We told him no, but said we had acquired a pair of meercats called Donald and Hogan instead. These two were already firm favourites with the public. We produced their credentials.

A young woman, who turned out to be a new officer of the Veterinary Department, to our dismay, took charge of Donald and Hogan.

"You can't bring them in without the usual six months' quarantine," she announced.

8

"But surely you are mistaken," protested Armand. "These aren't cats, you know."

"They are closely related to the mongoose," I added.

The young woman looked unimpressed.

"They will have to spend the night here," she said, making some notes in a little black book.

"In any case," I added hopefully, "cats and dogs, even if these were cats or dogs, which they are not, are surely allowed to enter Kenya from England without quarantine?"

It was no use. Calling over her shoulder that there was nothing that could be done, the young woman took poor Donald and Hogan away, and we heard the unfortunate animals scratching impatiently in their travelling box as they were borne to some remote room in the customs building.

"I'm so sorry," said our friendly customs official, sympathetically. But I assured him that we would telephone the Veterinary Department on the following day and certainly be able to secure Donald's and Hogan's release.

As the African boys at the airport were carrying our baggage to the car park they urged us to tell them what we had been doing in England. "Did you enjoy it?" "Was it hot?" "Was it cold?" "Was there much food?" But before we could answer any of their questions we were greeted by an old friend, Mike Richmond, who had come to meet the plane and drive us to the New Stanley Hotel.

We had known Mike for many years and had often flown in his private plane. It was always difficult to imagine that this slim, rather boyish-looking man had lent both his single-engined aircraft and his personal services to the Police Reserve at the outbreak of the

9

Mau Mau troubles and for three long years had constantly undertaken the most hazardous reconnaissance missions. There had been three other young men under his command, but two of them had lost their lives in operational sorties. Mike himself was a born flyer, with just the right amount of caution to balance his innate daring, and it was this quality that had made him a first-rate test pilot for the Fleet Air Arm during the last war.

In a few sentences he told us all the latest news—especially in so far as it concerned our house, which we had lent during our absence to a couple called Winkelmeyer, who were local car agents. It seemed that they were shortly to be transferred to Uganda, which meant that our property would soon become vacant once more.

"Well," said Armand, "that means we'll have to find a caretaker."

Tentatively, I voiced a suggestion. "Don't you think it would be nice," I said, "if we could live in our own house for the first time even if it's only for a couple of weeks?"

We had owned the land on which the house was built for ten years, and for nine years the house itself had stood there, yet we had still never spent a night under our own roof.

Armand laughed. "I'm afraid you're getting the nesting instinct," he said.

This was true enough. How many times during the past few years had I fallen in love with some place where we were camping and said, "Let's stay here for ever." It might have been in the depths of New Guinea or in the heart of Africa—but it always had plenty of trees and birds and animals—and scarcely any people. It was not that I disliked human beings, but cities and

10

populated areas always give me a feeling akin to claustrophobia.

At the New Stanley Hotel we were welcomed warmly by the European staff and the African boys, all of whom had known us for many years.

"We have only managed to book you in for two days," said a beautiful Danish receptionist, when we enquired after our accommodation. "We did try to fit you in for longer somehow, but there's a convention on at the moment." Her eyes registered sympathy. "I'll do my very best," she said. "Let's hope there will be a cancellation."

"We ought to have let them know earlier, Armand," I said reproachfully. But before the words were out of my mouth I realized how unjust I was. We never knew with certainty when we would be on the move, and during most of our married life we had been unable to tell from one moment to another where we would be the following week. It was always difficult to arrange any sort of social life, and even the ordinary business of booking hotel accommodation was invariably a speculative operation: fortunately we were both fairly adaptable and it did not worry us overmuch.

"We had better not unpack everything," said Armand, when we had moved into our suite. "They may want us to move into other rooms in a day or two. Or we may even have to change hotels."

"Armand."

He looked up. He knew from my tone of voice that I was going to suggest something I wanted very much and was already afraid that he might refuse.

"Well, what is it?" he asked. "I know what you're going to say, and the answer is——"

"You can't really know what I'm going to say."

"The answer is 'yes'."

"You really mean it? We're going to move into our own house?"

I ran across and kissed him. This was too wonderful for words! I felt ready to start moving there and then.

*   *   *

I hope my readers will not think me guilty of exaggeration when I say that our house at Langata, a few miles from Nairobi, is one of the loveliest I have ever seen.

We built it on the edge of a quarry that slopes down to the Mbagathi river. On the far side of the river is the Masai Reserve and in the distance we can see the Ngong Hills and the matchless splendour of the giant Kilimanjaro.

Around the house, the cropped lawn ensures that snakes do not trouble us overmuch, and a border of gorgeous lilies—my favourite flower—adds a magnificent touch of colour. In the grounds, the trees are chiefly natives of Africa: fig trees, flowers of the forest and thorn of various sorts, with roses to remind us of England in June and jasmines to waft a heady perfume over the house.

If I close my eyes, I can always hear the gentle ripple of the river and smell the sweet scents from the woods, however far I am away from home.

Armand designed the house, which is a white Moorish-style building with terra-cotta roof tiles. Inside, the central feature is a large wrought-iron staircase of a delicate, leafy design, made to my own drawing by an Indian craftsman in Nairobi.

But the house is unusual in another way. With such a view, we decided to reverse the conventional way of building and have our living room on the first floor and bedrooms and bathrooms at ground level. At the

12

top of the house is our writing room—a disadvantage, as I have since discovered, for who can concentrate on words when the majesty of nature distracts at every season?

This was our house, without furniture or servants, the place I was eager to turn into a home.

The terrorists were still active, and our first need was a nightwatchman. Fortunately the Winkelmeyers had not yet dismissed their own nightwatchman, and we were glad to keep him on. His name was Kirmani. He was a tall, elderly man with one of the most beautiful African faces I had ever seen. His eyes were slanting, his cheek-bones high, his nose was straight and thin, and his expression like a carving from antiquity. It could have been the face of a saint, an ascetic or an Egyptian king. He was considerably taller than I, and when he looked down at me, it was in the manner of a man whose womenfolk have no franchise. We engaged him on the spot.

Armand and I went to the storeroom and unpacked our safari cooking-box, which contained plates, cutlery, and kitchen utensils. Our army-style ware looked appallingly incongruous in the grandeur of the house but it would have to do. While Armand and Des Bartlett, his assistant, who had just arrived, did the unpacking, I went to the nearest provision shop, which was two miles away, and bought food.

When I got back I settled myself in the kitchen at the top of the house and started peeling potatoes: but a moment later I practically jumped out of my seat. Out of the corner of my eye I had seen a motionless figure standing just inside the doorway.

It was Kirmani.

Without a word he came forward, took the knife from my hand, and started peeling the potatoes. I had not asked him to help me in the house at all, and I was consequently very touched by his action. Having thanked him, I left him to the potatoes and busied myself with making a special sauce for the fish I had bought. I was determined that our first meal at home should be an especially good one.

*   *   *

I could scarcely believe that we were really in the house at last. Although it contained practically nothing beyond our camp equipment, in my mind's eye I could already see it furnished.

Armand had said, "I built the house. Now you buy the furniture."

I was only too happy to do so, for it put on me the responsibility of making a real home. My pleasure was a trifle dampened, however, when I discovered just how much our dream house was going to cost to furnish. To make the most of the breath-taking views all around us, Armand had designed a house with many windows. But it was not until the upper floor had been measured for curtains that I realized, to my horror, that I would have to buy no less than a hundred and fifty yards of curtain material. In fact, I bought sixty yards to start with, but then had to wait a further six months for the remaining lengths to arrive from France.

Buying the furniture and carpets was fun until I worked out how much they were costing me. Every day I totted up the bills and groaned, but each new piece I acquired injected extra life and personality into the house. It had suddenly become the same to me as a beloved person. I wanted to give things to it—to dress it up and make it beautiful. Even Armand, who had originally shuddered at the sight of the building's bleak interior and referred to it as Grand Central

14

Station, viewed my efforts with increasing approval. At first, everything had seemed to go wrong, but the arrival of my blue-grey curtains which would not fade in the tropical sun cheered me considerably. Finally, after I had haunted auction sales in Nairobi, the furnishing and decoration were completed, and Armand announced that he was satisfied with the result. Visitors always admired our home, but it was naturally Armand whom I really wanted to please and I was delighted to have succeeded in doing so.

There were of course problems still to be overcome. In a downstairs cupboard I discovered a beautifully coloured nocturnal mouse which I fed and cherished. With nine cats in the house, its survival was always in doubt, but by making sure that no one opened the cupboard except me, I managed to preserve the mouse. But one morning, as I was sweeping a precious prayer rug, I noticed a triangular piece had been nibbled away from one corner—obviously the work of my nocturnal pet.

I thought of my other carpets: the Aubusson tapestry in the living-room, the Bokhara purdah on the floor of the writing-room and other Persian carpets in the house. Sadly I went downstairs to the cupboard, caught the mouse, and liberated it well away from the house.

During those early days when we were settling in we lived a camp-like existence. Almost every day I was to be seen driving a vehicle which looked almost like a furniture van, with oddly shaped parcels, bundles, packages, lamps, and the legs of chairs and tables jutting out of the back seat.

In the house Kirmani helped by preparing the vegetables and washing up, but otherwise I did all the housework myself as well as my writing and filming. I congratulated myself on Kirmani's extraordinary conscientiousness, for he had the knack of anticipating whatever needed to be done without being told. Very often I went into the kitchen and found him hard at work all on his own, and at night he sometimes used to prowl around the grounds on the lookout for Mau Mau. He seemed to be that rarest of commodities—the perfect servant—and I considered myself extremely lucky. "He's a treasure," I often exclaimed to Armand.

One day I went to the kitchen as usual to prepare lunch and was mildly surprised to find that Kirmani was absent. However, I presumed that he must have decided to take the day off, and did not give the matter a further thought. Lunch was served, I did the washing up, and then changed into my film clothes for some sequences we were shooting that afternoon.

But in the evening there was still no sign of Kirmani and I began to feel a little worried, for I had visions of him having been spirited away in the night. After dinner, I mentioned his absence to Armand.

"Oh, he's probably gone off with some friends," Armand replied.

"But he should have told me," I said.

"Kirmani is old enough and big enough to look after himself."

However, I could not rest until I knew whether or not he had returned to the servants' quarters, so I went across to see for myself. The door was locked, the building was in darkness, and there was no reply to my knocking. I was alarmed and quickly returned to the house.

"Armand," I called, "he's not there."

"Who?"

"Kirmani."

"All right," said Armand, "we'll enquire at the

16

Ride a rhino
—two versions

The author

Nugu, the colobus monkey, and the vervet were inseparable

Woven gourds are part of a Somali wife's bottom drawer

police station tomorrow. Perhaps he's had an accident. Or maybe he really has been beaten up by terrorists."

Next morning Armand walked across to the servants' quarters to see if there was any sign of Kirmani. A few moments later he returned to the house.

"Your devoted servant," he announced, "is lying dead drunk on his bed."

I was bitterly disappointed, for I had always defended Kirmani's character. He could not be roused until the afternoon, whereupon he sheepishly apologized and promised that it would never happen again. In stern tones, Armand forgave him, and I presented him with a couple of aspirins for his hangover. He assured us that he would turn over a new leaf—but two days later he again strayed from the path of virtue.

"Perhaps he's lonely," I suggested. "Or maybe it's a social habit. You often find Europeans who drink through loneliness. I think we should employ some other boys, Armand. He needs company—and I could do with some more help."

"I don't want any boys at this time; we can't tell who is Mau Mau and who isn't," replied Armand.

However, I pleaded that I needed more time for my writing, and I finally succeeded in having my way. That afternoon I visited the nearest Labour Exchange. A cook and a houseboy were quickly found, and on the following day they reported for duty at the house. The houseboy seemed to be quite a cheerful little fellow, but the cook looked lugubrious beyond words.

"I wonder if he ever smiles," said Armand, when we were alone. "Or will our soup be drowned in tears?"

Nevertheless, the household thenceforth ran more smoothly, allowing Armand and me a chance to give all our attention to our respective jobs. Kirmani, however, continued to have his occasional lapses, and it was perfectly obvious that his avowed intention of turning over a new leaf stood little hope of ever being fulfilled. After a while I got to know all about his drinking habits. There was, for instance, one infallible sign: he would always try to acquire or ask me for an onion. The first time this happened I was combing my hair in front of a full-length mirror in a small dressing-room on the ground floor. It was dusk, but I had not bothered to switch on the lights, for I could just see what I was doing. Suddenly, as I gazed at my own reflection I became aware of a dark, motionless figure peering into the mirror over my shoulder. There had been no sound of approaching footsteps, and I swung round sharply.

It was Kirmani.

"What do you want, Kirmani?" I demanded, in a rather severe tone, for my nerves were on edge. Armand had gone into Nairobi for the day, and Kirmani and I were alone in the house, and thoughts of the Mau Mau were never completely out of one's mind at that time.

"Would you give me one onion, please, memsahib?" he said, in a thick voice. At that time, of course, I did not realize that this was a sure symptom of his alcoholic thirst, so we went to the kitchen together and I gave him an onion.

After that, it happened quite regularly.

One evening, when Dr Louis Leakey and his wife Mary were having cocktails with us, we caught sight of Kirmani creeping up our large central staircase. We can see from one end of our house to the other through a succession of archways: but Kirmani was quite oblivious of the fact that he was being watched. He crept up with elaborate caution, and then we heard faint sounds of exploration from the kitchen. Mary and Louis raised their eyebrows.

"I'd better go and investigate," I said, feeling rather annoyed. It was all right, I considered, for Kirmani to creep in and ask me for an onion when I was alone, but to do so in front of guests seemed to be going too far.

I found him rummaging about in the vegetable basket.

"What are you looking for?" I said, although I knew perfectly well.

"One onion."

Kirmani was reeling, and his hand described a wavering arc as he took the onion which I found for him. I left the kitchen and returned to my guests and to my surprise, instead of using the back stairs, he followed me. However, I considered it prudent not to object at that moment, for I felt I might get rid of him much more quietly by just letting him creep down the main stairway and out of the front door.

I entered the drawing-room, and to my intense annoyance Kirmani followed closely behind me. He walked into the centre of the floor, where he stood swaying like a blade of grass in the wind, and gazed fixedly at my guests. Then he raised his arms and waved, extravagantly, in an all-embracing gesture.

"It is a beautiful house," he announced, employing the sort of tone you might expect from an exalted personage conducting a party of week-end guests around his ancestral manor.

"Very good furniture," he continued, crossing to a window and fingering the curtains. "Very good material."

He then wandered into my writing-room, but he was soon back again. We pointedly ignored him.

"Yes, it is a beautiful house," he repeated, his eyes sweeping the room from floor to ceiling. And with those words he shuffled off down the staircase, munching his onion and steering an unsteady course for the front entrance.

When he had gone I apologized for the unorthodox behaviour of our watchman and we all laughed. There was very little you could do about Kirmani.

One evening Armand and I were going out to dinner in Nairobi. Des had also been invited, but had decided to stay at home instead to write some letters. As we were getting into our car we saw a Nairobi taxi pulling into our drive, so we waited a minute. The cab stopped at the house and out of it stepped two young African ladies. There was something familiar about their mincing walk. Where had I seen it before? Piccadilly? Shepherds Market? Bond Street? Yes, it was familiar.

"I suppose they've come to look at our animals," I said. "Or perhaps they are the boys' sisters?"

"They don't look like anybody's sisters to me," replied Armand, who had obviously also recognized their gait.

Since Des was in the house and could protect our belongings, it seemed unkind to order them off the premises if they had merely come to see the animals, so we drove off to our dinner-party.

It was about midnight when we returned. The first thing we saw was the bobbing of a torch outside the house. We could feel at once a strange tension in the atmosphere which seemed to suggest that something peculiar was happening or had just happened. The bobbing torch approached us rapidly, and we soon recognized the figure of Des dressed only in a pair of shorts.

"The police are here," he called.

"Mau Mau!" I spontaneously exclaimed.

"No," he replied. "Girls."

We asked for details, and he told us that there had

evidently been a terrific fight in the servants' quarters. The police had been sent for, and our entire household staff, with the exception of Kirmani, had been carted off to gaol. We were to take Kirmani down to the police station on the following morning for interrogation.

As far as Des could gather, the fight had been caused by an argument as to which members of the staff were to be privileged to enjoy the favours of the two girls, both of whom had fully intended to spend the whole night in the servants' quarters. In his role of *askari*, or nightwatchman, Kirmani had thereupon gone to the police-post on his own initiative and brought two policemen back with him. Des knew nothing more except that the cook, the houseboy, the garden boy, and both the girls had then been taken to the police station.

Kirmani, it appeared, had convincingly vindicated himself—a most timely action, because he had lately been indulging too frequently in drunken bouts and I had been seriously considering giving him notice.

The next morning, soon after breakfast, I drove Kirmani down to the police station and the interrogation began, each man being questioned separately.

It is always most entertaining to watch Africans being interrogated. Their natural dramatic talent is given full rein and they enact their roles, whether truthfully or not, with such vivid actions and descriptions that the whole scene comes clearly to life. In this instance all the boys, who had been kept in separate cells during the night, told more or less the same story. The girls had been lavish with their favours to all three of them, but Kirmani had been ignored because he was a Wakamba. For some reason neither of the girls could tolerate the Wakamba tribe, and Kirmani's passionate advances had accordingly been rebuffed. A lively fight among the men had ensued, and all four of them had suffered considerable and visible damage. Kirmani had then, in a fit of jealous pique, gone straight to the police station and reported the incident.

I was astonished at his duplicity. There was nothing for it but to dismiss both him and the cook, who had been responsible for bringing in the girls. The cook had not been in our employ long enough for us really to miss him. He was a good cook, but I knew I could easily hire another. We did soon find another, a light-fingered gentleman who lasted in our service no longer than his predecessor. Finally I almost came to the old conclusion that the best cook for our kitchen was myself.

The sacking of Kirmani was a different matter. I felt really unhappy to see him go. He may have been a rogue, but he was extremely pleasant. Drunk or sober he always amused me, and I do not think I ever employed a servant with so much character. Wherever he is now, I wish him well.

CHAPTER TWO

THE LIMPING LION CUB

IT seemed—and was—ages since we had been on safari and we were delighted to be on the move again. Since our return from England, we had been busy with all the many things which have to be attended to whenever we come back to Africa.

When we planned our new safari we took with us two African boys who came more for old times' sake than through need of a job. Kamando and Njogu were men of some substance who each owned a sizeable *shamba,* or plantation.

Kamando had worked for us many years previously. Prudently he had saved money and had been able to retire: but he liked us and regarded us as friends, almost relatives, rather than employers. He loved safari and was quite happy to work as cook-houseboy, while Njogu was content to lend him a hand in camp and to drive one of the jeeps. Usually African drivers do not care to do any other job as well, but since Njogu had often seen me peeling potatoes or helping to change a tyre, and Armand doing many odd chores which were not his normal responsibility, he showed his readiness to help in every way he could.

We set off in two vehicles—Armand and I in a truck and the two boys following in a jeep. A week later Nairobi was far behind us and we felt ourselves in another world. We pitched our camp beneath the spreading branches of a large flat-topped tree, a species known in the old days as the "fever-tree" because the early South African pioneers imagined that it was the direct cause of fever. Perhaps the sickly yellow of its bark originally gave rise to this idea. Whatever the reason, for many years it was blamed for what we now know is the work of the mosquito.

We had put up two tents—one for ourselves, the other for the boys—for this was lion country and we did not care to risk sleeping in the open. The risk of lions actually is small, the greater danger being a nip from a foraging hyena. Armand once told me that he had slept all night under a tree and next morning discovered the fresh tracks of elephants all around his camp bed. A lion can obviously penetrate the flimsy canvas walls of a tent with ease, but rarely does so unless it is a man-eater . . . and a lion does not turn man-eater unless he is injured.

That night, in our tent beneath the big fever-tree, with a river running close at hand, Armand and I lay listening once more to the exciting chorus of Africa's nightly orchestra—the croaking of frogs, the woof-woof of the hippos, and the chilling laugh of the hyena. There was a sudden scuttling sound across the canvas roof as the feet of some small animal, possibly a rat, raced frantically to escape the attentions of a nocturnal hunter.

With the pressure-lamp hissing on the table between us, both Armand and I held open books in our hands: but neither of us read a single word, for we were too thrilled at being out in the wilds again. I do not remember Armand turning out the lamp. Suddenly I opened my eyes and saw Kamando in the tent.

"Tea, memsahib," he said.

Outside it was cold and grey: but as soon as we had finished breakfast and were getting into our vehicles the sun made a sudden appearance and lit up the still half-sleeping earth. The greyness of the sky gave way to a deep blue across which white clouds of rare luminosity rode in splendid array.

We drove through the coarse golden grass in which the antelopes were already feeding. They gave a momentary start as we drove by, then continued eating —an uncommon reaction in a territory which was not a National Park. As a rule the animals are terrified at the approach of man, for the safaris of so-called sportsmen have made the human race a feared and detested enemy. But the part of the country to which Armand had brought us was off the beaten track and not easily accessible.

Suddenly a fantastic sight presented itself. As we were driving close to the animals we unexpectedly ran over a boulder and Armand's elbow inadvertently pressed the horn. The impala—those antelopes of infinite grace with lyre-shaped horns—leaped into the air, and the entire herd started cavorting like a corps de ballet. They circled and leaped in such fashion that one soon ceased to wonder at the ancient Greeks with their legends of Winged Pegasus, for these antelopes were surely in flight, their feet hardly seeming to touch the ground. Then, as we drove away, they came suddenly to a standstill and gazed at us rather self-consciously after their display of panic.

Whenever we came to a clump of thick bush we gazed into its deep shadows, for we knew that was where we were most likely to discover the king and his family. Often, after a gargantuan feast, a pride of lions would lie stretched in the coolness of places such as these until hunger drove them to make another kill. We usually reckoned that a pride would go hunting no more than once in three days.

We drove a long way and there was still no sight

nor sound to indicate the presence of a single lion in the territory. But as our hopes were beginning to dwindle, we drove through a circular mass of tangled trees and were confronted with a sight which made us catch our breath.

"Look!" said Armand in a whisper.

There they were; three lionesses and seven cubs.

The beasts saw us, and one of the lionesses crouched and lashed her tail. She then gave a little mew which sounded harmless enough but was nevertheless an unmistakable warning to us not to come any nearer.

We noticed that, of the seven cubs, three were slightly larger than the rest. As we watched, three of the smaller ones ran towards a lioness who was lying in a crouching position. The fourth small cub followed at a distance, but we were unable to see it clearly. The others, meanwhile, came up to their mother, nuzzling against her with a touching show of affection, and one of them rubbed its little face against hers just as a kitten would. It was almost impossible to believe that this gentle mother could become a savage and fearless killer if aroused.

Then, as we watched this charming little family scene, the fourth little cub came clearly into sight.

"Oh, Armand," I cried, "he is injured!"

The cub's left hind-leg was swollen, and the fluffy little creature limped painfully towards its mother. It looked much thinner than its brothers and sisters. We watched it as it lay down beside the lioness, resting its head upon one of her huge paws and closing its eyes with an expression on its cuddlesome face of mingled weariness and utter contentment. With even more tenderness than she had displayed towards the other cubs, the lioness licked first its face and then its

26

left hind-paw. A cut was clearly visible in the swollen, fleshy pad, and although the wound was partially healed it had obviously festered.

"If we could treat it with penicillin," said Armand, "we could probably save it."

"We simply must do something," I said. "But how can we lure it away from the others?"

"It's impossible," he replied. "And unfortunately we can't explain to its mother that we could fix it up in no time if only she and the others would move a little distance away."

I sat in silence, distressed beyond words at the sad fate I envisaged for the wounded animal. With their highly developed family sense, the lions had not deserted the little cub; but it was almost inevitable that the wound would become rapidly gangrenous and be eaten into by maggots. The stench of an animal so afflicted is too dreadful for any sensitive person ever to forget.

"We should come back here tomorrow," said Armand, who had been filming some close-ups of the lionesses and their cubs. "We know where they are and they look fairly well fed. I doubt if they'll go hunting tonight. In any case, they couldn't move far with that wounded cub."

Back in camp that evening the thought of the injured cub haunted me.

"Armand," I said, when we were drinking coffee after dinner and discussing our programme for the next day, "don't you think we might try to separate the cub from the others when we go back to the lions tomorrow?"

He asked me how I would propose to do it.

"If we took the jeep as well as the truck," I suggested, "we might be able to split them up." Perhaps,

I thought, if we waited until they got used to our presence we might find an opportunity to separate them.

Armand did not think a great deal of the idea. "It wouldn't be easy," he replied, "but it may be worth trying."

Next morning, we told Njogu to follow us out in the jeep. We made straight for the spot where we had last seen the lionesses with their cubs, and sure enough, with the exception of two of the adults, they had scarcely moved.

We sat in the car and watched the antics of the seven cubs under the watchful eye of the remaining lioness, who lay crouching in the shade in stately splendour like one of the stone lions in Trafalgar Square. We circled around them a couple of times, then switched off our engines and settled down to see what would happen.

After an initial uneasiness and air of suspicion, the animals seemed to grow accustomed to our presence. We were not too close, yet near enough to see everything in perfect detail. As the morning wore on, the lioness would occasionally utter a sleepy yawn. Her eyelids closed, and her head would nod, falling gradually lower and lower until she would suddenly awaken with a start.

"Why doesn't she relax and enjoy her siesta properly?" I complained to Armand. And at that moment, as though she had understood my words, she rolled on to her side and fell fast asleep.

The cubs went on playing together, and even the little one with the wounded paw tried to join in, but was forced to retreat to a safer distance when the hurly-burly became a bit too rough.

"Let's try to grab him now," I suggested eagerly.

"Shall we get Njogu to drive the jeep between him and the others?"

"I think it's too soon," said Armand. "They aren't quite used to us yet. But we could try."

We started up the engine and signalled Njogu to do likewise; but instantly, as though suspecting our purpose, the little cub limped hurriedly towards its mother and flung itself beside her.

We shut off our engines, and, still watching, drank the coffee and ate the sandwiches we had brought out with us. For a while the cubs went on with their game. Presently one of them, evidently intent on scaring its mother, edged slowly forward, crouching on wobbly legs, and prepared itself to spring. Whereupon the others, not to be outdone in this stalking game, converged on the unsuspecting lioness. And as they surrounded her, the first one sprang.

The reaction of the lioness was so like that of a domestic cat that we burst out laughing. With her tail lashing in mock or genuine anger, she cuffed the first cub and dealt with the others in just the same fashion as any of our own household cats would have done. But, unfortunately for us, her action had no greater effect upon the cubs than that of a mother-cat upon her kittens; it merely served to incite them to further attacks, adding spice to their game, until she had been fully roused and was as wide awake as ever. Despite her obvious annoyance, however, her patience was astonishing, and she remained remarkably gentle even when her offspring and their playmates landed with their full weight on her stomach.

She tried in vain to resume her siesta; but suddenly she sat up, and as she did so all the cubs stopped romping and pricked up their ears. We had heard nothing. But then, suddenly, we saw the tall grass

29

rustle far end of the clearing and another lioness, perhaps the mother of the smaller cubs, stepped silently into the open. As she came forward, the first lioness rose to meet her, for all the world like a hostess greeting a guest, and the two of them circled around each other, rubbing faces and purring. Now the four smaller cubs trotted up to greet the returning lioness with a great show of affection which she reciprocated with loving indiscrimination. It was obvious that she was their mother, and that the other lioness had been doing an hour or two's baby-sitting—or, rather, "cub-sitting."

The two families then started to move off, but the little cub with the injured foot was left limping far behind. Before we could make a move, however, its mother stopped, turned, waited for it to catch up with her, and unceremoniously picked it up by the scruff of its neck with her teeth. It looked a frightening business, but the little cub seemed perfectly happy and even curled itself up so that its feet would not drag on the ground as it was carried along.

"Where do you think they are going?" I asked Armand.

"Perhaps they've made a kill," he replied. "Let's try and follow them."

If they had made a kill, the male lion or lions would almost certainly be in the vicinity, though we knew it was possible for the lionesses to hunt on their own.

Usually, when hunting, the males roar and drive their quarry towards the waiting lionesses, who lie in ambush. We have watched lions hunting many times and are always struck by their extraordinary co-ordination of thought. As if to a pre-arranged plan, they each make for a seemingly appointed position and move forward with uncanny telepathic understanding until one of them makes the last fatal spring. It was astonishing to see how they always moved at precisely the correct pace, each perfectly and strategically placed as though the whole operation has been carefully discussed beforehand. And, as sometimes happened if the unexpected occurred, it is surprising how they react in unison, as if they were in radio contact with each other.

The lionesses and their cubs now moved forward and we travelled slowly behind, halting every now and then so as not to alarm them by getting too close. But it was sometimes difficult to keep them in view because their colour blended so perfectly with the golden scenery.

After a while the lioness carrying the cub paused to lower her burden. She looked round panting and surveyed the scene with that faraway gaze, like all cats when they are not on the prowl. This was good, for if ever a cat focuses its eyes upon a particular animal it usually indicates an immediate and unhealthy interest.

We had drawn close enough to the lioness to see that her paws were bloodstained. Flies were swarming around her mouth and eyes, so we knew she had recently made a kill. She started to wash her paws and stroke her face in the manner of an over-sized house-cat.

"This might be our chance to try to get the small cub," said Armand.

We beckoned to the jeep behind us, and moved slowly and cautiously to within a short distance of the lioness and her cub. As Njogu drew level with us we told him in a stage whisper what we wanted him to do. Before setting out in the morning we had already discussed a plan of action, and when we gave Njogu the word, he knew that he was to try to drive his jeep between the lioness and her cub. We would then drive alongside the little creature and attempt to pick it up. It was a dangerous plan, but we reckoned we stood an even chance of bringing it off. The element of surprise would be in our favour, but if the lioness stopped to pick up the cub we knew we had no hope of success.

We gave the sign. Njogu raced towards the lioness and we followed close behind. Startled, she looked up and snarled, being taken by surprise she involuntarily retreated two or three paces. The next second Armand had leaped out of our truck and was no more than a yard from the little cub when I suddenly saw a movement in the grass behind him.

"Armand!" I shouted. "Get back!"

For a split second he hesitated, torn between the overwhelming desire to pick up the cub, which was now so tantalizing near, and the instinctive need to heed my warning.

Mercifully he stopped, and without panic clambered back into the truck. But he was only just in time. As he regained his seat the second lioness sprang. She had returned, undoubtedly to see what had happened to the others, and I had luckily spotted her as she emerged from the long grass. The lightning speed with which she had stopped short in her tracks and sunk on her haunches, her honey-coloured flanks twitching as the muscles tensed for action, was a sight that filled me with terror. Armand had left the engine ticking over, and as he pressed the accelerator the truck leaped forward as if it, too, were stung by fear of the lioness. I felt physically sick, far more frightened than if I had been in the same danger. I must have looked white and shaken, for Armand patted my arm.

"It's all right," he said. "I'm still here."

With Njogu following close behind we made a wide detour, and it was some time before we sighted the

Armand with the genette cat and Bertram the bush baby

Jean Lathbury

Trespassers on Gannet Island

A small part of the vast colony on a sea-lion island

lionesses and the cubs again. But by now the desire to follow them had been largely stifled, for we both realized that there was practically no chance of saving the little cub.

Under a large, flat-topped tree there lay the partially devoured carcase of a wildebeeste watched over by a recumbent lioness. Several vultures were perched on the branches above her head, while on the ground, at a respectful distance, two or three jackalls waited, their keen, pointed little faces registering intense watchfulness in case the lioness dozed off for an instant and gave them a chance to steal a share of the kill. But although the temptation to relax her vigil must have been great, the lioness faithfully guarded the banquet for the others.

In the thick bush beyond the tree we could discern the majestic outlines of two maned heads, one black, the other golden. And as we watched, the black-maned lion released a prodigious yawn, shook his mane, closed his eyes, and rested his head sleepily upon his paws. Then, as though he found yawning as infectious as we do, the other lion yawned as well. To my great amusement, I noticed that Armand, too, was yawning in sympathy with them.

As the lionesses and their cubs came up to join their lords, there was a lavish display of affection on all sides. After that the bigger cubs and the lioness who had not yet eaten strolled over to the carcase beneath the tree and settled down to gorge themselves. A large portion of the wildebeeste's stomach had already been devoured, for lions invariably start eating their kill between the thighs, on the soft part of the lower belly. But there were still plenty of titbits left for the late arrivals.

When they were replete they all retired to a shady

spot under the tree, and the golden-maned lion got up with a long stretch and a yawn, to take his turn in guarding the kill. One of the vultures emboldened by the fact that the carcase had been left momentarily unguarded, swooped down from its perch on the tree, but no sooner had it come to earth than the lion sprang forward and took a heavy swing at it with his paw. The discomfitted bird uttered a squawk of alarm and, leaving some feathers fluttering in its wake, wasted no time in returning to the safety of the branch. It settled among its fellows, resigned to a long wait.

Eventually, when it became evident that the lions were far too sleepy to entertain us further, we reluctantly decided to strike camp and go on our way. We had enjoyed staying with our pride of lions and felt almost as though they had become old friends—in spite of the manner in which our intentions towards the little cub had been misconstrued.

"If only," I said to Armand, "if only we could have convinced them that all we wanted to do was to heal his foot. . . ."

Our camp, which had been of the simplest, was easily packed and our gear quickly stowed away on the following morning. Our route to the next camping site took us past the large, flat-topped tree where we had last seen our lions, but when we reached it there was no sign of them. I had been hoping to catch a last glimpse of them and perhaps—who knows?—to steal a last chance of saving the little cub. Nothing was to be seen except a seething mass of vultures. As we drove up close some of the birds broke away and we saw the white ribs of the wildebeeste glinting in the sunlight, picked as clean as though the carcase had been boiled for several hours until the flesh had fallen away. One vulture was standing in the cage of ribs, from which vantage point it was able to stretch upwards and, relatively unmolested by the others, pick minute particles of flesh from the underside of the neck.

Some little distance away, as we moved on, we saw a jackal proudly running along with a trophy between its teeth. It reminded me of a pet dog sent out to fetch the Sunday papers and delightedly carrying them home. We recognized the jackal's spoils to be a leg of the wildebeeste and were happy to see that a substantial amount of meat still remained on it. The jackal was probably taking this dinner home to its family, so although one victim had been sacrificed, many had eventually benefited by its death. Nature may often appear to be cruel, but there is a logical pattern behind its apparent ruthlessness. It is the human hunter we hate who kills either for money or to inflate his own ego.

I often wonder what these seekers of thrills, these so-called he-men feel about our own life of adventure, in which we have never found it necessary either to kill or to carry a gun. Our greatest protection lies in our knowledge of animals and in our ability to recognize the danger signals. We have often been charged by fierce animals, and I suppose a hunter in similar circumstances would have shot to kill, justifying his action by saying that he had been obliged to protect himself. But Armand and I are still alive because knowledge is often the most effective protection against danger in the jungle and the bush.

Four months passed before we returned to the territory where we had last seen our pride of lions. I had often thought of the poor little cub, but had long since given up hope of its survival.

As we drove along, an impala sprang with a soaring leap out of our path, and three wart-hogs, with tails erect, scuttled off into the tall grass. Armand slowed down.

"Look, Michaela," he said, pointing to a column of vultures in the distance. "Something's been killed. Let's see what's going on."

We drove off to where the birds were congregating in the dark blue sky. This was one of the problems we have never solved and never cease to marvel at. How can the African sky at one moment be an enormous blue void, and at the next be speckled with a converging multitude of scavengers?

Slowly circling overhead, the vultures formed a great column which gradually, speculatively descended to the earth. Often in the past, through following the descent of vultures, we had located lions with a recent kill. And so it was now.

As we drew close we could see three lionesses, three cubs of almost adult stature, and four smaller ones, all gathered around the kill.

"That must be *our* pride," I cried excitedly.

From what I could see none of the smaller cubs was limping, but there was no doubt at all in my mind that these were our lions. This was their territory; their size and numbers were exactly right; but the final and most convincing proof came when the group was joined by two males; one had a golden mane, the other a black one. Lions were so scarce in this part of Africa at that time that we knew beyond a shadow of doubt that this was what we had come to call "our" pride of lions. The mother of the small cub must have tended its paw so diligently, nursing it and constantly cleaning it, that nature combined with maternal devotion had cured it completely. The little cub did not limp now, nor was he in any way physically inferior to his brothers and sisters.

As we drove away I glanced over my shoulder to catch a last glimpse of the lions. I saw a friendly family party gathered around their dinner. And my heart rejoiced at the knowledge that no member of the household was missing.

CHAPTER THREE

TO THE FRONTIER

ONE of the most interesting and unspoiled areas of
Africa lies to the north and east of Kenya: the land
of the Somalis and the Boran, of the camels and the
great brooding deserts.

Here, too, lions are found. As I have said, lions do
not become man-eaters unless they are old or injured,
but when that happens, they turn to human beings as
the easiest of all kills. Without a weapon, a man cannot
fight even an old or wounded lion; he has no hooves or
claws or sharp teeth to protect him and he cannot run
away. When a lion turns man-eater whole districts can
be terrorized and hunters have to be brought in to
kill the rampaging animal. One regrets the necessity,
but it is the only way with a lion who has declared war
on the human race.

On an expedition to the northern frontier we joined
forces for a night or two with a white hunter who had
been called in to track down a man-eating lion. The
lion had become so bold and his partiality for human
flesh so great that he would raid a thornbush enclosure
to get at the goats and then, ignoring them, would seize
the herdsman sleeping among them and carry him off.

The chief at the village through which we passed
brought out a girl who told an extraordinary story.
She was about fifteen years old, good-looking and well-
made, but her dusky features were marred by several
long claw marks which ran down one side of her face.
She told us that she had been tending a flock of goats

on the outskirts of the village early one morning when the man-eater had sprung out on her.

"It knocked me over before I realized I was in danger," she said proudly. "For some reason it did not bury its teeth in me at once, but stood clawing at me as I lay on the ground—perhaps to make sure I was dead. As I rolled over with the lion panting over me, I groped for the stick I'd been holding—then suddenly I had it and threw it as hard as I could against the lion's jaw. It was so surprised that it backed away—and just then some men from the village came running up and drove the lion off with their spears. I was lucky that time, memsahib."

Not only lucky, but brave. Word had gone round that the white hunter with us was to kill the lion and all day warriors had been arriving at our camp. They had magnificent bodies and their fine features and high cheek-bones gave them the look of strong, fearless men.

An enclosure of thorn was built at night round the camp fire for protection, and after the men had eaten meat which they grilled on sticks, they began a lion dance, foretelling the death of the enemy. The grunting and shouts of the dancers drowned the night cries of the hyenas, and as I watched the rippling muscles of the warriors gleaming in the firelight and listened to their blood-curdling threats of what they would do to the lion, I wondered why it had been necessary to send for a white hunter. The warriors seemed confident of finishing the job themselves.

The dancing and eating went on all night, and as dawn broke, the hunter and the warriors made ready to track the lion. With the white man at their head the warriors set out. Armand and his assistant had decided to go with the expedition in the hope of getting pic-

tures, but I stayed in camp. Even if the lion was a man-
eater, I could not bear the thought of him being hunted
and killed in cold blood.

The chanting of the warriors died away as they disappeared in the distance. The sun rose, and as I had
plenty to do, time passed quickly.

Occasionally I gave a thought to the lion and once it
crossed my mind that he might escape the hunters and
decide to pay a visit to the undefended camp. But I
soon dismissed the thought. Late in the afternoon I
saw the warriors coming over the hill in single file with
the hunter and Armand at their head. Their return
was strangely dejected, compared with the excited and
bloodthirsty sally of the morning.

"Did you kill the lion?" I asked when the leaders
reached the camp. Armand gave a derisive hoot and left
the hunter to tell me what had happened.

"You heard what the warriors were going to do to the
lion this morning?" he said. "Well, when we got into
the country where we know the lion is, their bravery
evaporated. They wouldn't fan out and beat so as to
give me a chance of a shot when the lion broke cover.
Instead, they insisted on walking behind me in single
file because I had the gun, and we've been walking in
single file ever since we left camp!"

I was reminded of this episode—by no means typical
of African behaviour, I hasten to say—as we now
travelled towards the frontier.

We had left Mount Kenya, with its barbed-wire
barricades, its road-blocks, and its native Home Guard,
far behind us. Armand and Des Bartlett were travelling
in the Queen Mary, our three and a half tonner, while
Malawa, our boy, and I followed in the Power Wagon.
Presently we arrived at Isiolo, gateway to the Northern
Frontier District, beyond which one cannot pass with-

out permission, for the passage of irresponsible people who might get lost or cause trouble is discouraged.

At Isiolo, we stopped to call on the Provincial Commissioner, Noel Kennaway. I have always been immensely impressed by the outstanding qualities of Provincial Commissioners in Africa. They seem invariably to be remarkable men, and I imagine they are selected for the qualities which include, not only a thorough knowledge of native language and customs, but also humanity, humour, sensitivity, and the ability to cope with any situation.

Such a man, we found, was Noel Kennaway, who greeted us at the door of his bungalow and invited us to tea. His home was cool and spacious, with pale green polished floors overlaid with good Persian carpets, tastefully furnished and charmingly decorated. It was a gracious home, and although Mrs Kennaway was on holiday in Europe I felt instinctively that I would have liked her on sight, for the stamp of her personality was to be seen wherever one looked. Noel himself had very blue eyes, dark hair, and a beautiful voice. We all took an instant liking to each other.

It was after we had been chatting gaily for a while at the tea-table that I heard a peculiar squeaking noise from the region of Noel's stomach.

"Poor man," I thought. "He must be suffering from indigestion."

Armand, who had obviously heard the noise, too, did his nonchalant best to ignore it. We continued talking and laughing—but still the squeaks continued. Then, suddenly, a small head popped out of Noel's shirt.

I started laughing—for it was the face of an extremely familiar animal.

Noel glanced downwards. "Ah," he said, "the Kennaways pet mongoose!"

Presently Noel's son, Tony, a boy of thirteen, joined us with two of his friends, Robin and Christopher Tyler, who were fifteen and twelve respectively. The mongoose scuttled delightedly towards Tony and tried —extraordinary though it may sound—to climb into his mouth. This, apparently, was a favourite game of which he never tired.

The three boys, Noel told us, were the greatest of friends, and it seemed from their manner as though they had not a care in the world. But those were trying times for parents, for Mau Mau had been active in the country and several white children had already been murdered.

"I have a trusted old Somali who keeps an eye on the boys," said Noel. "He would give his life for them— and he is always armed."

When later I talked to the boys themselves I realized that they were fully aware of the danger around them, but they possessed the true courage and adaptability of youth and the threat of Mau Mau did not seem to worry them at all.

After tea we went to the guest house, a mud and wattle building thatched with large leaves, which was some distance away from Noel's bungalow. Around us, as far as we could see, there stretched the dusty golden landscape. It was a blustery afternoon, and every now and then we saw a dust-devil whipped up by the wind, rising like a spinning top as it whirled upwards into space.

We settled ourselves in the guest house, and later visited the shopping district at the far end of Isiolo, patronizing the first *duka,* or store, which was owned by Hadji Abdulla Farah. To all outward appearances, the *duka* was like many others, stocked with all sorts of general merchandize. Boxes of chocolates jostled with oil-lamps: rolls of vividly coloured cottons, of which the Somali women are especially fond, were stacked alongside piles of canned foods and sacks of coffee and rice; cardigans and reels of cotton stood next to trays of medicines, lipsticks, hair oil, and notebooks. Everything likely to be needed for a journey or for day-to-day living was available, and in addition there were enticing strings of beads which the Turkhana would use for embroidery on their costumes. As we entered, two Turkhana girls were haggling over the price of some ultramarine beads, and a fine-looking old man with the light skin of the Somali and a long henna-dyed beard to indicate that he was one of the Faithful who had been to Mecca, gazed at us with idle curiosity.

Hadji Abdulla Farah, the owner of the *duka,* came forward to greet us. He was a tall man—as tall as, if not taller than, Armand, who is very tall—and he carried himself with dignity and modest self-assurance. His English was flawless.

We ordered generous supplies for our journey, for we knew that our route would lead us through semi-desert where people have barely enough food for themselves. On such journeys as we were about to undertake we never attempted to buy provisions from the natives, for we knew that they might be tempted to go short of food which they would exchange for cash or goods.

The purchases completed, I ventured to compliment Hadji Abdulla on his command of English.

"Were you at school in England?" I asked.

He smiled slowly. "English is no problem for me," he explained. "My father was Irish. Perhaps you knew my brother who died recently?"

He mentioned his brother's name, and I had indeed known him. I now realized who Hadji Abdulla was.

His father, a titled man, had married a very beautiful Somali girl, who gave birth to the Hadji; but after a few years he had divorced her and married again, this time a European, by whom he had another son. After his death, Hadji Abdulla had never claimed his birthright, and his younger half-brother had inherited the title.

I said that I considered Hadji Abdulla's action in waiving his rights to the title both noble and generous.

He shrugged and again smiled his slow, gentle smile. "The title meant nothing to me," he said, "but to my brother it meant a great deal. I am quite happy living with the people of my mother."

I then asked the Hadji if he could do us a favour. We had been unable to take Mucharia, our old cook, with us. We had not been able to trace him, but before setting out I had met a former servant of ours (who had set himself up in his own business since leaving our service and had become a man of considerable wealth), and learnt from him the sad news that Mucharia was being held prisoner as a Mau Mau in McKinnon Road Camp. It grieved me to think of our former cook as a Mau Mau, but many strange things happened during those days.

Newly arrived troops who did not speak Swahili had made a number of understandable mistakes, and any typical Kikuyu was in danger of being picked up. Mucharia, because of his filed teeth, had been unmistakably Kikuyu and I thought he might easily have been arrested by mistake: but what made the thing more sinister was the fact that his entire family had also been imprisoned in McKinnon Road Camp between Nairobi and Mombasa. It was difficult to imagine that an entire family innocent of terrorist activities could have been imprisoned. But then, I had been thinking

44

along the same lines as practically every other European in the country—it was inconceivable that your own "boys", whom you regarded as part of your family, had been treacherously inveigled into taking oaths to maim you, steal your possessions, or even kill you.

We knew that had happened, though, of course, there had been many exceptions. Our brave Malawa, I knew, had defied the Mau Mau, and I had insisted on continuing to employ him although it meant filling in innumerable forms and whenever we entered a town, constant vigilance to see that he was not picked up by the police or military because he was a Meru—the Meru, Embu, and Kikuyu tribes being the chief Mau Mau supporters.

So I asked Hadji Abdulla if he could find a cook for us and perhaps a houseboy. He thought for a moment. "I know of a very pleasant young man who is anxious to go on safari, but I don't know if he can cook," he said. "All I can say is that he's a very willing worker. Perhaps you would like to try him?"

I thought it would be a good idea, whether the boy could cook or not, for I enjoy cooking and have taught many boys. I consider cooking to be one of the arts and, like most arts, it is better when one's pupil has no preconceived ideas.

About two hours later a tall, slim, and handsome young Somali, named Mohammed, was introduced to me. He wore a turban, a spotless white shirt, and an elegantly draped *kikoye*, a long piece of cloth bound round the waist, which fell to his ankles. We spoke in Swahili which I had learned at the rate of five new words a day until I had a good vocabulary—when I first went to Africa. He admitted at once that he knew nothing about cooking, but I said I would teach him.

That evening Mohammed came back to the guest

house with us; and later, in the kitchen, which was contained in a separate building, I gave him his first cooking lesson. The kitchen was small, with a stove of ancient design in one corner, and was lighted only by a single oil-lamp and the red glow of the fire. Malawa helped me to prepare and cook the meal, while Mohammed, I hoped, was taking in all that he saw us do.

When we had put on several pots to simmer and there was nothing more to be done but to wait, I thought I would ask Malawa about his experiences at the hands of the Mau Mau. I was not at all sure that he would be prepared to talk on this subject, especially since Mohammed was new to us; but I was glad that he agreed without hesitation, and in the red glow of the firelight the menace of Mau Mau became suddenly and frighteningly real. Malawa told his story simply in a beautiful, modulated voice, and the whole terrible picture was brought vividly to our eyes. Mohammed, who was casually peeling potatoes, would stop whenever the story became very dramatic, and gape with knife poised in mid-air and his horror-filled eyes unblinking and incredulous.

"It was late one night," said Malawa. "There were just four of us in our hut when there came a knock on the door. I opened it and saw a man, whom I knew, standing there with some other men behind him. They pushed past me and closed the door behind them—as though to shut out other eyes. My wife picked our child from the floor, and my mother moved out of a dim corner of the hut so as to be nearer the fire.

" 'You are one of us,' said a man whom I did not know. 'You are Meru.' He was a Kikuyu, and when he spoke even the man I knew kept silent. 'Tonight you will take the first oath,' he said.

46

"I did not ask him which first oath. I knew only too well that these men were Mau Mau and that they had forced their way into my home. I thought of the massacres for which they had been responsible, and even as I saw my own small child huddling to its mother's breast I could not help thinking of those other children who had lain beneath the dead bodies of their parents. An overpowering shame came over me.

"'No,' I said, 'I will never join you. If you go away now, quietly, I will not betray you. But I cannot become one of you. I am a man of peace.'

"As I spoke, their faces were filled with hatred. One of them seized my old mother. While three others held me back, he grabbed her old thin arm and dragged her towards the door. Then they extinguished the light so that only the embers of the fire lit up the scene. The door was thrown open. I heard a ghastly thud—the sound of steel tearing through old flesh and hacking through brittle bone—followed by one agonized, piercing scream. Then again there came the terrible chopping sound, a whimper that became a low moan. Then nothing but the sound of chopping. I cried out with horror in a voice that was not my own.

"The murderer came in, and the dark red glint of blood on his glistening skin was caught in the ember glow. One of the men seized my child from his mother, leaving a deep crimson smudge across the white blanket covering him. I managed to struggle out of the grasp of the men who were holding me and seized the child in my arms.

"'Do what you like to me,' I cried. 'Cut off my arms and legs!'

"One of the men snatched a glowing timber from the fire and jabbed it against my leg. But I was so wild with horror and sorrow that I was unaware of pain

47

until I smelt the singed flesh. It was then that they demanded for a second time that I should take the oath. I nodded my head. I scarcely knew what I was saying or doing. My lips made their responses and my body went through the unspeakable things that were demanded of it. Like a brainless corpse, I had taken the first oath. The door closed, and I suddenly found myself alone again with my wife and child.

"At daybreak I went out of the hut. My mother's body had been dragged away, and a pile of newly turned earth showed where she lay. My soul was filled with hatred. My mother, who had given me milk, had sacrificed her life for my child, my wife, and myself. She who had been so patient, who had toiled all her days, whose forehead had borne the mark of the strap which had supported a million burdens on her back, had ended her life at the hands of these butchers. I loathed them, these men of madness, more even than I feared the death and torture of myself and my loved ones."

Malawa paused, his forehead glistening with sweat at the memory of that terrible night. "I forgot to mention," he said at length, "that they had cut down all my corn and maize and had ripped our clothes to ribbons and stolen all our money."

He told us the worst things first, as though to purge his soul of them.

"The past is past," I told him, touching him very softly on the arm to bring him back to reality. "Your mother is not dead. She lives in you and in your work against the Mau Mau, and her spirit watches us." What I had said I indeed felt to be true, for in the dim light of the kitchen there was no doubt that the spirit of the old woman was so close as almost to be tangible.

Her son continued; "That very morning I went

48

straight to the police. They took me to see the District Commissioner. I told him what had happened—that I had been forced against my will to take the first oath—and that I was prepared to fight this terrible thing in every possible way. After that, whenever the Mau Mau strangers came to hold meetings or visit their friends in our village, I was always accepted as one of them, and my wife and I used to go and listen to what was discussed and decided. And on the following morning the District Commissioner and the police were always informed what had happened. Often, when the police raided our district and made some arrests, no one would be prepared to give evidence against these men, although many people had seen them plot and execute their terrible deeds. But my wife and I used to give evidence—in a secret court."

I was forcibly reminded of the last sentence in my book "Leopard in my Lap"; *Courage is life, fear and be slain*. I did my best to translate these words into Swahili, very badly I am afraid, but Malawa and I were so much *en rapport* with our mutual sense of horror that he seemed to understand exactly what I meant.

Our dinner was very late on the table that evening.

CHAPTER FOUR

LOCUSTS AND GHOSTS

WE drove towards the semi-desert which lies in the heart of the Northern Frontier District, passing through a belt of scrub and stunted trees. No European had travelled along the road for two and a half years and as bandits were active in the area, we were provided with an armed guard.

There was beauty shimmering in the sunlight. It was not the opulent beauty of lush vegetation but a pinky gold vastness that stretched as far as the eye could see. There was beauty too in the jagged outlines of extinct volcanoes which jutted like black, irregular teeth on the skyline. Here nature is implacable and God does not help those who do not help themselves. Water is life and the peoples of the region have been skilled at well-building for many centuries.

We stopped to watch men at work drawing water from a well which went down deeply into the bowels of the earth. Standing on narrow ledges cut at regular intervals in the well-shaft, men swung the leather bucket upwards with a precision it was a delight to watch.

The man in charge of the team was old but he was still strong and upright in spite of his grizzled appearance. He stood at the top of the well and led his team in an old rhythmic chant. The words were taken up all the way down the shaft and the sound made by the singers was strangely haunting. Time and time again, without fumbling, the bucket was passed from hand to hand and as soon as it was emptied into the trough at the top, it slapped to the bottom again with a dull thud.

"Did you notice anything about the leader of the team?" asked Armand after we had watched for some time and prepared to drive on.

I looked again. The old man was completely blind.

We drove on, and had only just entered the belt of scrub and trees when there was a sudden sharp tap on the windscreen.

"Locusts," said Armand, for he knew that where there is one there will always be many more. Within a moment the windscreen was being spattered by a hail of them, and several came flying through the windows. They looked like giant grasshoppers, swollen and heavy with the vegetable matter they had eaten, and I began to throw them out by the dozen.

We closed the windows, to within an inch at the top, but still the insects hurled themselves like buckshot against the glass and piled up against the windscreen. The road by this time had been practically obliterated by a crawling mass, and Armand's car, which had gone ahead, had left its wheel-marks imprinted on millions of squashed bodies. Soon the road was so quickly covered that we lost sight of it completely.

We stopped the car. Armand and Des had already pulled up in front of us and were scrambling out. As we opened the doors the insects flew into our faces, bombarding us at such a speed that they stung. Both Armand and I had waited for a long time to photograph a locust invasion, for although we had seen several in the past we had never managed to secure any pictures of them.

"Look, Michaela!" cried Armand, pointing to the

stunted trees which were literally blanketed with insects.

There was something frightening and yet awe-inspiring about the purposeful, relentless onslaught of these millions of mandibles. The boughs creaked under their weight, and only the skeletons of trees were left when they passed on. Watching them, I could not help saying to Armand how similar they are to our own species. I realized with a shiver that unchecked humanity, with its ever-increasing fertility, could destroy the entire earth just as inexorably. The locusts are now controlled by an international organization. Could not humans be controlled in the same way before they destroy themselves?

These were my thoughts as the cameras were set up, and Armand and I moved forward into the seething mass. With every step we took, a fountain of insects soared up before us. They got into our hair and crept into our shirts and trousers. We had to stop constantly to pull them out, for although they are harmless, their prickly legs are maddeningly irritating to the skin.

We moved into the thickest patches, and as we stood there, pelted by this hail of flying bodies, we saw branches which had actually been broken by the weight of the insect armies. It was a fantastic, almost unbelievable, sight.

"Are they good to eat?" I asked Armand.

He laughed. "Hungry again?"

I was not particularly hungry, but I remembered that we had once eaten locusts in Uganda. They had been quite small—no more than two inches long—whereas these were at least four inches in length and much plumper and heavier.

"Personally," said Armand, "I wouldn't care to eat them. I'm told they often have internal parasites—

large white maggots. Besides, they're not very appetizing."

The appetites of the birds, however, were not in the least blunted. They hovered on the fringes of the invading hordes swallowing locusts as fast as they could.

We knew the chief of Locust Control in Kenya, which wages a ceaseless war on locusts. We visited him on a memorable occasion when a vast swarm, to whose extermination he was dedicated, had descended on his own front garden and systematically devoured his favourite rose-bushes.

"A raid on enemy headquarters," Armand had said, laughing.

The Control does great work. Its policy is to locate locust swarms when they settle after one of their great flights and to destroy them with insecticide, sprayed from the air. Fortunately an insecticide which is not harmful to birds has recently been discovered, for in the past great multitudes of birds were unwittingly poisoned—a dual tragedy, since birds are the natural enemies of locusts and consequently play a vital part in controlling the menace.

When we were back in the truck and on our way to Garba Tulla, we passed an empty bungalow which reminded me of one of the most curious things that had ever happened to me . . . and my life has certainly not lacked out-of-the-way situations.

"Do you remember the Browns?" I asked Armand. "That's where they used to live, I think. How desolate it looks."

He looked blank for a moment, then nodded, smiling gravely.

"That was certainly an odd business," he said slowly. "But you've no proof. No one would believe you—unless they knew you."

"I have proof, Armand; it's at home in the files. But never mind, let's not argue about it."

For the rest of the journey I sat and thought about that extraordinary happening. It must have been about a year ago when I first met the Browns. A nice couple, the husband in a government job, the wife settling quickly into the life of the country. I had been introduced by an old lady, Mrs Partridge, who had always enjoyed our television programmes in England and had written to me to say so. When she came out to Kenya to visit her son we often met and had become very friendly.

We were having tea one day in Nairobi when Mrs Brown and her husband called. My friend showed them a signed photograph I had given her, at her request, and Mrs Brown at once asked whether she could have one, too. I, of course, agreed to send her one and soon after rose to go. Months passed. Armand and I had a great deal of work to do, another safari to arrange, and my promise was forgotten.

Then, six months later, I was back in Nairobi. It was a hot, bright day, just before noon, and the streets were crowded. I was hurrying along to make a few last-minute purchases before driving home for lunch when a man stopped me. I have a good memory for faces, and after a moment I recognized him as Mr Brown. We shook hands and he asked how I was.

"Fine, thank you," I replied. "How are you? How is your wife?"

He looked worried. "She's going through a difficult time just now," he said. "She badly wants cheering up. You know, I think it would help her if you'd be good enough to send that signed photograph you promised. Do you remember?"

I felt terribly guilty. "But of course! I'll do it right

away. I'm so sorry, but we've been so busy it completely slipped my mind. Now, are you living in the same place? I'm sure I have your address."

"Yes, she's still there. Many thanks, Mrs Denis, it's very good of you. You won't forget?"

"I'll send it straight away. Goodbye, and do give her my very kind wishes when you see her. I do hope she'll be better soon."

Then he was gone in the crowd, and I made for the shops and drove home. As soon as I got in I went up to my study and spoke to my secretary.

"I happened to meet Mr Brown in Nairobi just now and he reminded me that I'd promised to send a signed photograph to his wife—apparently she isn't well. It was months ago, and I forgot, I'm afraid. Will you write a little note for me and send this photograph off right away? I'll sign it now."

I dictated the letter, and the photograph was sent off that same day. For a week I heard nothing. Then, when I was on another visit to Nairobi, I met Mrs Brown, much to my surprise. On impulse I went up to her.

"Hallo, Mrs Brown! How are you? Did you get the photograph?"

She looked pale and drawn, and I remembered her husband's words. She smiled wanly.

"The photograph? No, I haven't had it, Mrs Denis. When did you send it?"

"Last week. To the address you gave me. Your husband——"

She bit her lip.

"I've been away for a week or two. Haven't you heard about my husband, then?"

I looked blank and, with an effort, she went on: "He's dead, Mrs Denis. He died three weeks ago. I

55

simply couldn't stay on alone in that bungalow, so I've been with friends."

I stared at her, and felt myself go pale. I badly wanted to sit down.

"Dead?" I repeated stupidly. "But—when, did you say?"

"Three weeks ago. He went very suddenly; the heat, you know. It's given you a shock, Mrs Denis; I'm so sorry to have to spring it on you like this." Her obvious concern made me pull myself together. What was I to do? Tell her I had met and talked to her husband a week ago in this very street, as solid and alive as any of the people walking past us now? As alive and human as she herself?

I could not. It would not be fair to give her such a shock, and it might well have a very serious effect indeed. I knew from experience how differently people reacted to death, and I would first have to find out her views before subjecting her to any further pain. I managed to say goodbye, and, cutting short my visit to the town, drove straight home. As I went along in the car I could not believe what I had seen and heard. I went over every detail of Mr Brown's conversation with me; saw again in my mind's eye his solid, flushed face, the stocky body in some light-coloured jacket and trousers. Felt again the firm, warm handshake. And yet his wife—who should know—had said that he had been dead for three weeks. So he had come up and talked to me about the photograph, in full daylight, in a crowded street, about ten days *after* his death!

When I arrived home, I went straight up to my study and spoke to my secretary.

"Do you remember my telling you about meeting Mr Brown in Nairobi a week ago?"

She looked up, then said, "Of course, Mrs Denis.

56

You do look troubled. Is anything the matter? Didn't the photograph arrive?"

"Mrs Brown's not been at home for some weeks. Have we a copy of the letter?"

She handed it to me and I scanned it quickly. There was no mention of my meeting her husband. But it had been sent on that same date.

Slowly I went down to lunch. Over the meal I told Armand about it. He took an objective interest in the odd things that happened to me from time to time, regarding psychic phenomena in the same detached and scientific manner in which he approaches everything else in life.

After listening in silence he said at last, "But Michaela, if the street was crowded, surely someone must have seen you either talking to this man in the flesh, or else talking to yourself or to the empty air. Did you notice anyone glancing curiously at you?"

I shook my head. We were used to being stared at in the streets. I would not have noticed if anyone looked round at me, and I told Armand so.

"Did he walk up to you, or did he just materialize?"

"He came towards me, through the people, along the street."

"You shook hands?"

I nodded.

"When he went, did he just vanish?"

"Armand, I don't know! He turned and went away. I didn't take all that much notice. I hardly knew the man, anyway, and I was thinking about my shopping! I wish *you* could explain it, for I can't although I accept it as fact. I've known too many strange things in Africa—and all over the world—to discount the fact that a dead man can return in spirit to the living."

Armand smiled at my vehemence. "I know your

beliefs, Michaela. But let's try and prove it, shall we? Now, did you see anyone else that morning?"

I shook my head. "I have the letter I wrote to Mrs Brown when I came home. I told my secretary straight away. That ought to be proof enough."

Armand pursed his lips. "It might have been an hallucination; perhaps you felt guilty about not sending the photograph."

It was no use. Something strange had happened to me one hot noonday in Nairobi and people would have to accept or reject it, according to their beliefs. For me it was real, and merely another proof of that greater world that lies all around us, if we have eyes to see. Anyway, that deserted bungalow on the way to Garba Tulla reminded me acutely of that strange experience. It is one I shall never forget.

CHAPTER FIVE

SCORPIONS GALORE

WE were still reminiscing over that strange experience **as we** drove along the road to Garba Tulla. This grand name is given to a small collection of *dukas* which exist to cater to the needs of the nomadic Boran and Somali. Here they come to buy beautiful cottons for their womenfolk, and sandals, made from old tyres, for themselves. Europeans holding administrative posts occasionally pass through and pick up supplies.

Mr Pereira, the owner of one of the *dukas*, received us hospitably, and treated us to long cool drinks which were just what we wanted after the heat of the journey. Refreshed, we strolled through the village to see what it had to offer photographically.

The Boran women wear strikingly beautiful costumes, which consist of a single length of cloth knotted at the back, draped over one shoulder, and secured at the waist. Many of them wear necklaces of large beads, rather like amber, while others are adorned with silver ornaments and bracelets. They have almond eyes, thin classical noses, high cheekbones, and skins like peaches in both colour and texture. The men are extremely tall, most of them at least six feet and more, and wear their thick black hair upswept and rounded like haloes. For the most part they are bare to the waist, but wear lengthy measures of cloth wound around their hips.

A chief of the Boran named Galmadida arrived as we were shopping for supplies. He had met us once before and had promised to come and see us in Garba Tulla. He possessed strikingly classical features, and with his great height and a large geranium-coloured turban he looked every inch a king. To our delight he asked us if we would care to visit his encampment—an invitation which we quickly accepted.

Before leaving Garba Tulla we called again at Mr Pereira's *duka* and asked him if, in our absence, he would try and collect some scorpions for us. The store owner was greatly perplexed by our request until we explained that we wanted to photograph them. He went into the main part of his shop, where a large crowd of Somali was assembled, and announced that he would pay a reward for every scorpion brought in. This statement caused considerable mirth among his audience, who wisely consider that scorpions are best left alone, but when I added a few words of explanation the laughter stopped and the request was taken seriously.

It was already late in the afternoon when we set off for the encampment. We did not keep to the road, and the going was rough. Our route was strewn with boulders, and often we came to patches of sand in which we might easily have been bogged down. On these occasions our guide would obligingly hop out and walk slowly in front of the truck in order to test the ground.

Eventually we arrived at our destination—a group of beehive huts made of matting. Or perhaps I should describe them as tents rather than huts, for they are entirely portable, being made from hoop-like sticks over which the matting can be draped in a matter of minutes.

The warmth of our welcome by these nomads was truly touching. When they heard the sound of our trucks the men came running from the thornbush barricade which encircled the encampment and helped to guide us across the difficult terrain. We had to negotiate a dried-up river-bed—no easy manoeuvre in the semi-darkness—and our friends were lavish with directions and counter-directions as to which was the best way to cross. One would suggest that it would be easier to go to the left, another was convinced that the safest way was to the right. But whichever direction we chose, we seemed either to run straight into a patch of thornbush or to find ourselves perched perilously near the brink of a sheer drop. Finally, however, in the face of a spate of good-natured argument among our guides, we safely reached the confines of the encampment and were greeted by the muted tinkling of scores of wooden camel bells as the animals roused themselves at the noise attending our arrival.

We were all tired out after our hard day's driving and our only wish was to get into bed as soon as possible and we decided to camp outside our host's encampment. But first there were numerous jobs to do. Armand and Des cleaned the cameras and equipment; Malawa checked the oil, petrol, and water in the vehicles; Ali went foraging for firewood, while Mohammed first filled and lit the lamps, then helped me to prepare a meal of eggs, bacon, and sausages fried in butter. We were all thirsty, but had to wait half an hour while our water-purification tablets dissolved and took effect. Even so, this was a far quicker way of getting a drink than the old method, of boiling the water for ten minutes and then having to wait for it to cool.

After our meal in the open air we settled down on our camp-beds beneath the star-speckled dome of the African sky. To sleep like this was to enjoy a feeling of peace and freedom such as one never experienced in a city. I closed my eyes in perfect contentment and knew no more until I was awakened next morning by the mingled sounds of lowing cattle, bleating goats, and tinkling camel bells.

First of all we wanted to photograph the life of the women in the encampment. When we had washed and dressed, we wandered into the enclosure and soon made friends with some young women who were busy about their work. Although they were all Moslems, they were not in purdah and were at liberty to move about quite freely.

One of them invited us into her home; the circular, tent-like dwelling looked wonderfully cosy inside. Beautifully woven water-carriers and gourd-shaped vessels, decorated with cowrie shells and supported by leather straps, hung from posts or the walls. The floor had been stamped so smooth that it looked almost permanent.

There was a captivating fragance about the hut, and I could not resist asking the girl where it came from. She pointed to a square wooden board supported at the corners by blocks which raised it slightly off the ground, and crouched down to lift the lid. Beneath it I could see a cavity in the earth containing some charred embers, and as I bent over the hole a pungent, heady, oriental perfume rose from it. The girl took down a little flask from the wall and showed us how, every morning, she poured the perfume over the embers so that the mats and all the contents of the hut became permeated with its scent. She was an intelligent girl and I asked more questions. She told us that the beautifully woven water-carriers and containers were part of a bride's bottom-drawer or hope-chest. We asked to see how these incredibly fine yet sturdy vessels were made, and she beckoned us outside to another enclosure which contained three more circular huts. There she introduced us to two women, to whom she explained that we would like to be shown how they went about their craft.

These women were wearing black cloths over their heads which totally enveloped their hair, showing that they were married. Their costumes, which were draped over one shoulder only, rather resembled elegant evening gowns. One of them was dressed in vivid scarlet cotton, while the other wore a design of purple and yellow stripes. Their almond eyes looked up at me in friendly welcome as they motioned me to sit down and watch them weaving.

They soon noticed how fascinated I was by the skill of their intricate work, inviting me to sit beside them and try my hand with their surprisingly simple-looking tools. To their delight I managed in a clumsy way to execute two or three stitches, and within a matter of minutes a number of other women gathered to watch the fun. They were openly amused at the sight of a stranger so awkwardly trying to practise this traditional art which for them was an everyday affair. However, it had one unexpected result! One old lady hurried into her hut to fetch a small vessel to show me. It was the finest example of weaving I had seen, and I warmly congratulated her upon her skill. On hearing my compliments she was suddenly overcome with shyness and hid her face with her hands, her laughing eyes peeping over her finger-tips.

From woven vessels we progressed to the wooden type in which camel's milk is kept. The Boran and Somali live mainly on this milk, and I asked how it was kept fresh. A demonstration followed. A piece of smouldering wood was placed in the vessel, shaken about, and then tipped out. It is as simple as that—

and it also accounts for the agreeable smoky tang which can be tasted when one drinks camel's milk.

On the following day we watched the milking of the camels, and it was certainly not an easy job for the milkmaids. I had often wondered why two people were required to milk a camel, and soon saw why.

The camel's teats are tied up with raffia, because at milking time it is usually accompanied by its foal and the milk has to be carefully shared between offspring and the milking vessel. The camel moved slowly forward, followed by its foal and the two milkmaids. When they were ready, the girls pounced on it, untied the teats, and started milking. The little foal tried desperately to reach its mother, but it was kept at bay until one gourd had been filled. It was then allowed to come forward and drink until it was satisfied, after which one of the girls started to fill a second gourd. But she had not made much progress before the milk suddenly stopped flowing.

We learned afterwards that the camel can draw its milk up into its body, and that it is very difficult to judge exactly when the milk will be lowered again. This wastes a lot of time for the milkmaids, for the petulant animal often seems to be on the point of lowering its milk, but withdraws it again before anyone can reach it.

After watching the milking we were shown a newly born camel. It was only minutes old—a grey, huddled little heap being licked by its mother. And then we witnessed one of those unforgettable miracles. Assisted by a nudge from its mother's nose, the little creature struggled to its feet and took a few faltering steps. It was an astonishing sight. An hour ago it had not even been born: yet here it was, already able to walk. I knelt beside it and stroked its head and its long

Our lion cubs could drink gallons of milk a day

Marilyn, the vervet monkey, preferred a soft drink

graceful legs. Its fur was greyish in colour, not unlike a Persian lamb, and wonderfully soft to the touch. Presently a young herdsman came and picked it up. He draped its legs around his neck, took the weight of its body on his shoulders, and carried it off towards the encampment with its mother following trustfully behind.

After this incident I spent quite a few days trying to persuade Armand that our life was not complete without a camel, and that as we were now travelling through the land of camels we ought to adopt a baby one and have it sent down to Kenya. My arguments unfortunately met with no success, but I have not yet entirely abandoned the idea, and perhaps when we are old we shall yet see a pair of camels wandering around our homestead.

Later in the day, we saw something that astonished us. No one had told us that camels blew bubbles.

Imagine our amazement, therefore, when one of a group quietly chewing his cud suddenly blew out what looked like a giant wad of dirty pink bubble gum. Bigger and bigger it grew, until it became the size of a child's sausage-shaped balloon. We watched, fascinated, to see what would happen when it burst—perhaps it was an elaborate joke. But without a change of expression on that aloof camel-face, the balloon stopped growing, shrank, and all at once disappeared without so much as a pop. He had sucked it all in again.

We had apparently missed seeing an angry scene— the camel blows bubbles when annoyed.

Without their camels, the Somalis and Boran would die, yet in one way they treat them in an atrociously cruel manner. It was Armand who pointed out the patterns the natives had burned into the flesh all over the camels' bodies. We tried to discover why they did this. Was it for identification or decoration? We never succeeded in getting a positive answer to our question, but whether the practice was reasonable or not, it saddened us to think of the agonies the camels must endure as a result of this barbaric rite.

On the following day, we bade farewell to our hospitable hosts and returned to Garba Tulla, where we were met by Mr Pereira at the entrance of his *duka*. He was in very high spirits and greeted us with the splendid news that he had several captives for us—two or three large black scorpions and about half a dozen yellow ones, which seemed far more active than the dark variety. The Somali excitedly explained to us that the yellow ones were much better and fiercer and their sting was much more virulent. We had not, in fact, expected quite so many specimens to be added to our menagerie, but we never refuse to pay a reward we have offered. Each boy, then, was paid for his catch and we found ourselves in possession of nine or ten malignant arachnids.

Once again, our goodbyes said to Mr Pereira, we continued on our way, but we had barely travelled a hundred yards when a small boy came running towards the leading truck and shouted for it to stop .

Armand leaned out. From the power-wagon behind I could see his face in profile, and I noticed his jaw drop as a rather large tin was thrust by the small boy into his hands. Some words were exchanged and Armand gave the boy some money. I could see the little fellow's face break into a happy smile, and he skipped merrily away.

Before we moved off again I clambered out of my truck and ran forward to see what Armand had bought. "More scorpions," he said, without enthusiasm.

I asked him how many.

"Sixteen," he replied. "That makes a total of twenty-five. We are heavily outnumbered by the enemy."

I returned to my truck.

The scorpions were kept in large tins with holes drilled in the top. At least, that was the general idea, but things did not quite work according to plan.

Two or three days later, when we were camping in the middle of the desert, Mohammed and I were standing in the back of the Queen Mary having a discussion on what should be cooked for the evening meal. On this particular evening we decided on a dinner of curried eggs and rice. There was no difficulty about locating the rice, for its bag was unmistakable. But to find the tin of curry powder was more of a problem.

Owing to the bumpiness of the cross-country tracks which we usually had to follow, it was not uncommon for the labels on the tins in our large box of supplies to be scraped off or to come unstuck as a result of the constant friction. On safari, there was therefore usually a considerable element of surprise about our meals, for we would often find ourselves eating, say, apricots and cream instead of the intended and fully expected salmon mayonnaise.

"Now," I mused, "I wonder where the curry is . . ."

I delved into the box of supplies and pulled out several tins, but Mohammed shook his head at each in turn. Presently I produced one without a lid. It had obviously once contained cocoa, but was now empty, and I was wondering if we might not have used it for the curry powder.

"What was in this one?" I asked Mohammed, sniffing the inside of the tin. "Was it curry?"

"No, memsahib," he replied, shaking his head. "It was scorpions."

I dropped the tin with a clatter. "Scorpions?"

"Yes, memsahib," he explained, "they were travelling on top of the food-box, but with all the bumping and shaking the lid must have come off."

"But where are they now?" I demanded.

"I think," he replied, pointing into the depths of the food box, "they must be in there."

This was serious, for while a scorpion's sting is not usually fatal, it can make you ill for a few days and even affect your eyesight.

I pulled on my heavy gloves, which normally I use only when handling the most untrustworthy of untamed animals, and with them I managed finally to extricate the tin of curry powder. But of the scorpions there was no immediate trace, though they kept cropping up in the most alarmingly unpredictable fashion during the days that followed.

Next evening, for instance, Malawa unwrapped his bedding and found one of them squatting on the pillow. He called me to see it. The creature scuttled back and forth with its tail, where the sting is secreted, twisted viciously over its back, ready to strike if the opportunity arose. We had considerable difficulty in recapturing it.

On the following day I took a box from the back of the Queen Mary and casually sat on it. No sooner had I done so than Ali, who happened to be passing, suddenly grabbed my arm and yanked me to my feet. At first I thought he must have been chewing a bit too much quoto-myrrha and had become light-headed. A moment later I saw how wrong I had been. Ali had acted only just in time, for a murderous-looking scorpion with tail curved upwards was scuttling over the box upon which I had been sitting a second previously.

It was Armand's turn next. One of the scorpions decided to make its home in his shoe. Fortunately, Armand, as a matter of habit, shook out his shoes before putting them on—and on this occasion he was rewarded by the recapture of one of the fugitives.

We had decided to keep the largest of the black scorpions in solitary confinement, because it was extremely pugnacious and fought constantly with its two dusky companions. Armand asked me for a tin or box to keep it in, so I emptied out a cardboard box in which we normally kept torch batteries and handed it to him. He punched one or two air-holes in the lid, and the black monster was then popped inside.

"Now don't forget where he is next time you need a torch battery," Armand said, half joking, half in earnest.

Time passed, and we had already reached Wajir, when one of the boys asked me for a new battery for his torch. I went to the store-room and without thinking opened the lid of the battery-box. My fingers were already inside when suddenly I heard an ominous rattle. It gave me one of the biggest shocks of my life and I felt that my heart had missed a couple of beats. I withdrew my hand as though it had touched a live wire and slammed down the lid. Luckily, I was unscathed.

Practically all the scorpions had by now been recaptured. But their Odyssey was by no means at an end. A little out of sequence, let me tell you what happened to them.

Armand, Des, and I flew down to South Africa after we returned from the Northern Frontier region. With us, though unmentioned on the passenger list, went all the scorpions which had been recovered from the Queen Mary, as well as the occupants of the second tin which Armand had received from the little boy at Garba Tulla. Des wanted to see if any of them would mate and breed, but since none of us know quite how to determine their sex there seemed nothing for it but to take them all and hope for the best. We were particularly eager to get some pictures of a mother scorpion carrying her babies on her back.

In Cape Town Des bought a glass aquarium which provided the scorpions with a pleasant home. He put a thin strip of wire mesh and a sheet of plate glass on top of it, so we were able to keep the scorpions under constant observation.

Des kept them in his bedroom, which he also shared with Bertram, our bush-baby, while Minnie the mongoose and Hogan the meercat stayed in our room. We preferred to keep them apart in this way because Bertram was a nocturnal creature and the others were not. Both Minnie and Hogan were inclined to become annoyed when Bertram wanted to play with them in the middle of the night, so in order to avoid ill-feeling or fighting, Bertram spent his nights with Des. There was a lovely picture-rail in Des's room, and Bertram's favourite occupation was to hang from it and walk all around at ceiling level.

But in the middle of the night there was a fearful crash from Des's room. In jumping from the curtain-rail to the dressing-table, Bertram had knocked over a heavy piece of camera equipment, which in turn fell and smashed the sheet of plate glass on top of the aquarium. Des awoke with a start, but by the time he had put on the light and got out of bed to find out what had happened there was not a scorpion in sight.

Next morning Armand, Des, and I searched the room in vain for any trace of the fugitives. Then we started looking for them up and down the corridors.

While we were groping around on hands and knees a dear old lady approached us and asked if we had lost anything and could she help. We were at a complete loss for words, since we did not dare tell her what we were looking for. I cannot imagine what she thought of us.

We never found any of the scorpions, and for all I know their eventful journey continues in an unnamed hotel in Cape Town. Nor have we ever obtained a film of a mother scorpion carrying her babies on her back. I wonder if we ever will?

CHAPTER SIX

DUEL WITH A DUST-DEVIL

OUR journeys in the Northern Frontier District and beyond had been more fruitful than we hoped, but there were many other regions of Kenya we still wanted to explore. Some of the areas were familiar and had already yielded exciting television programmes, while others meant breaking fresh ground in search of new material. But wherever Armand decided to go, I always felt the same expectant thrill as we left our home and set out on safari again.

In Africa, nature's kingdom is vast and we knew that each journey we took, if it was not exactly into the unknown, was likely to bring new experiences and reveal unsuspected patterns of behaviour among the animals we had come to love.

One of the best ways of photographing wild animals is from a tree platform. A platform is easy to make with a few planks and ropes, and if you are endowed with enough patience, the results can be excellent.

We usually make our tree platforms near a waterhole or over a well-trodden game path in the jungle. There are a few simple precautions to observe. The tree must be the right height and it must not be inhabited already—for woe to the person in a tree which is infested with ants or bees.

It is wise, too, to have a rail round the platform, for when the tree bends with the wind, the sitter can become dizzy. Finally, the experienced tree platform sitter always includes a good book with the food, binoculars, and cameras, since waiting to photograph animals who never appear can be extremely boring.

Our camp in a remote spot in Kenya was some distance from the tree platform Armand had built close to a water-hole. He had been taking movies of animals at the hole, and the results had been so good that he thought it would be a good idea to take some still shots. But our cameras were back at the camp guarded by the only boy we had with us.

"Shall I go back and get the camera?" I asked.

"Certainly not," replied Armand, "it's a long journey and I know what you're like. If you saw a hippo on the way you'd stop to pat its head."

"You know I'd shoot straight up the first tree!" I retorted.

The subject of hippos was a family joke at that time, though the incident which had caused the joke was not funny when it happened. We had been photographing hippos, rhinos, and elephants in Uganda and were travelling slowly near a pool when Armand noticed that a hippo was following our jeep.

"Try to take a picture," said Armand, who was driving.

It seemed a good chance, and with my feet on the running board, I tried to focus my camera quickly. But before I could manage it, the hippo had drawn abreast, changed direction and was charging the jeep at full speed.

There was no time for me to get properly aboard again, but luckily the hippo hit the jeep's side a foot from my leg. The jeep shuddered at the impact. As a blow from a charging hippo can easily reduce a human leg to pulp I felt an enormous sense of relief as Armand stood on the accelerator and we left our pursuer behind. "No," said Armand now, remembering that lucky escape. "You stay here and I'll go back and fetch the camera."

He strode off, leaving me contentedly scanning the surrounding countryside through his binoculars.

Presently, between the trees, I heard a "woof-woof" noise repeated over and over again, and saw a large troop of baboons moving forward. All of them were busily searching the ground and looking for grubs under upturned stones. The babies were perched on their mothers' backs, while from time to time the big males paused to bark at one another. One mischievous youngster seemed intent on teasing all his companions, and I saw him scamper up to one of them, who was slightly smaller than himself, and try to prise open his jaws. Baboons retain their food in their cheeks until both pouches are filled, then prod their cheeks with their fingers in order to transfer the contents of the pouches into their mouths. The victim squealed indignantly and took immediate refuge on his mother's back. She bared her fangs at the youngster, and at the same time a fully grown baboon, attracted by the baby's protestations, came and clouted the young delinquent on the head.

It amused me enormously to watch the baboons; they behave so very much like human beings, but without any of the usual inhibitions.

An impala was strolling among the baboons.

As I was watching the antelope, the baboons continued to move forward and mingled with it as it grazed. They were slowly approaching the water-hole.

It was then that I saw something which had often been described to me, but which I had never quite believed. If only Armand had not gone to fetch the camera! One of the baboons had leaped on to the impala's back and was riding it as though to parody a

74

jockey on a horse. I imagined that the impala might take fright, but it merely glanced over its shoulder at its rider and continued grazing. Showing no sign of nervousness nor even of irritation, the impala carried on as though oblivious of the acrobatic performance which was being given on its back. Up and down jumped the baboon, riding bareback for a few yards, then leaping nimbly to the ground before performing some fresh antic. Finally they reached the water's edge, and both baboon and impala stood there side by side, drinking together.

The impala did not betray an antelope's customary nervousness when approaching a water-hole. Antelopes are constantly alert to danger from the larger carnivores, and it takes only the slightest sound to send them bounding away from the water which each animal craves. But it was obvious that the impala which I was watching relied implicitly upon the baboons. The baboon's senses of sight and hearing are acute. They are great alarmists, and voice their fears most audibly. Indeed, we have often seen troops send scouts ahead—two or three big males who go forward, taking advantage of every bit of camouflage and cover in true guerrilla fashion, and scan the ground ahead until they are satisfied that the coast is clear. The scouts then give a signal (precisely what it is we have not yet discovered), and the main body of baboons follows in their tracks.

Now, before my eyes, they remained for a while playing around the water-hole. When wild baboons drink they elevate their colourful posteriors and lower their heads until their lips touch the water; yet tame ones, if given a bottle or a cup, are quick to imitate our own way of drinking.

Presently the baboons departed, but they had not

been gone for long before the next visitors arrived at the water-hole. They were three wart-hogs who had brought four very small babies with them. Grazing as they moved, the wart-hogs slowly approached the water-hole, pausing at every few steps to go down on their knees and grub for food. The babies kept very close to their mother, and whenever she got off her knees they made a concerted rush to try to suckle; but before any of them could get properly started she went down on her knees again, sending all of them tumbling. One little fellow, however, was more tenacious than the rest. He clamped on to her like a limpet and was always dragged several yards before he could be persuaded to let go. Another precocious youngster had already learned how to eat from his knees like the grown-ups. In a little cluster they all moved on to the water-hole, where they noisily drank their fill.

I looked around me. In the distance I could see two or three dust-devils—great columns of dust moving in swirling spirals across the landscape. A small pencil of dust, perhaps only three or four feet high, would start spinning like a top, faster and faster until it whistled up to incredible heights.

I returned my attention to the water-hole. There was no longer an animal in sight—nothing to be seen except the heat shimmering on the parched face of the earth, and drowsily contented, I closed my eyes for a moment. I have never felt alone in Africa in the way that one can feel alone in a big city. There is reality and stability all around, unlike the panic and insecurity of the civilization which we of the West have made for ourselves—a terrifying and claustrophobic civilization, founded on the selfish conception of Man as God, which somehow makes one feel that one is heading for inevitable oblivion despite oneself and by one's own hand. As I dozed I thought—or perhaps I dreamed—"When I die, let it be in Africa or in some place where there are trees; and let it be by an act of nature, by something I can understand."

I do not fear death for what it is, because it is surely also an adventure—one of the greatest.

My head nodded heavily, and roused me. I looked down again at the water-hole. There was still not an animal in sight. Armand had been away a long time —or did it seem so because I had been asleep? I glanced over my shoulder. There were just two dust-devils whirling against the sky.

But then, as I watched, it struck me that there was something unusual about the foremost spiral of dust. It was tall, taller by far than the ones to which we were accustomed. This was no ordinary dust-devil. It suddenly reminded me of the giant twisters which we had seen in the Pacific when working in Australia and New Guinea: but here, instead of sea-spray, was a thick and mighty column of dust, awesome as it towered above the landscape. Its velocity, moreover, I judged to be much higher than that of the average dust-devil. I watched it, fascinated, as it mounted in a sweeping arc across the sky. It was quite near to me now—but not until I saw what it could do to a tree did I realize how dangerous it was. The tree, flat-topped and standing some twenty feet high, lay right in the path of the advancing coloumn and was suddenly engulfed by it. And then, as the twister swung drunkenly away, I saw to my amazement that the tree had gone. Within a matter of seconds two more trees in its path had disappeared.

It was dangerously close to me now. Should I clamber down and run? But where could I run to? There was neither shelter nor cover that might afford me the

77

slightest protection. I had no way of judging from which direction this lethal spiral of dust might approach, and by altering my position I might easily run straight into it.

Even as I was debating what to do, I saw it coming straight for the tree—my tree. I jumped to my feet and started to clamber down the ladder. Suddenly, when I was about half-way down, I heard a tremendous roar all about me, and I was almost blinded by the wind and dust which beat into my face. The tree groaned. I heard branches snap overhead, and one hurtled past me, ripping the skin of my cheek as it passed. I clung to the ladder desperately. It was too late now to descend and too late to climb up again. All I could do was to hang there, waiting to be transported into space. I could feel the warm blood from my cheek trickling down my neck. I coughed and spluttered and wiped my eyes as best I could. Finally, after what seemed an age, I dared to look over my shoulder. The whirlwind had passed. The giant coloumn of dust was moving away, leaning over in a great swirling arc to the left.

'You have as many lives as a cat,' I told myself. It seemed incredible that I could have escaped death by such a slender margin.

I continued to cling to the ladder. Everything had happened too suddenly for me to have realized the full significance of the desperate plight I was in, but the reaction left me shaking and chilled to the bone in spite of the burning sun. For a while I stayed exactly where I was, still clutching the ladder, and feeling weak and almost paralysed. But presently I forced myself to climb back to the platform, where I lay down with my eyes closed and my teeth chattering.

"Are you safe?"

It was Armand's voice from below. He sounded frantic.

"Michaela!" he shouted—and then louder, in desperation: "Michaela!"

I crawled to the edge of the platform and looked over.

"I'm all right, darling."

He clambered up the ladder and took me in his arms and kissed my face and hair and neck.

"I saw it coming when I was half-way here," he said. "It seemed to be going straight for the tree. . . . When it passed and I saw the tree was still there I thought perhaps you had tried to get down and been carried away with it. . . ."

He gazed at me, and tenderly touched my blood-stained face.

CHAPTER SEVEN

A SHOT IN THE DARK

NOT long afterwards we treated ourselves to a week's holiday—our first real holiday in over ten years.

We both needed a rest, and in an unguarded moment Armand said we would take a month. But work piled up, the month was whittled first to three weeks and then to two, and finally when we set off, we had only a week of leisure to look forward to.

We had been obliged to borrow a car because our own was laid up for repairs and our trucks were being overhauled. We had a fairly straight run before us to the home of friends, so we did not anticipate complications, although we were told that our route led us through a belt of bush which was reputedly a favourite Mau Mau hideout. I shall not disclose its precise location, for I do not wish to embarrass the elderly gentleman who became involved in our subsequent adventure, nor do I intend to divulge his real name.

The car we had borrowed was much more luxurious than the vehicles in which we normally travelled, and one of its added attractions was its extremely powerful acceleration. We felt, therefore, that if we were unfortunate enough to run into an ambush or were surrounded by a gang of terrorists we might stand a reasonable chance of escaping because of our speed alone. In that territory European civilians had often been attacked and cars shot at. One couple we knew had even been attacked in the Ngong Hills, which was a popular place for picnics.

It had happened like this. Several parties of Europeans had, like our friends, been enjoying the beauty of the sunset on these hills and were beginning to drift homewards.

Our friends then made a fateful decision. They wanted a last-minute cigarette before leaving. As the husband was replacing the lighter in the dashboard of the car, two armed Africans suddenly appeared from nowhere, one to each side of the car. Grimly they demanded money. Then, without waiting for a response, one of them swung his panga at the window, shattering the glass and striking the wife a savage blow on the arm. At once his companion attacked her husband from the other side. No doubt both our friends would have been killed but for the wife's presence of mind. Despite her injury, which was now spurting blood, she managed to start the car and step hard on the accelerator. Her prompt action certainly saved their lives, but the injuries they received were so severe that it was many weeks before they were able to leave hospital.

No wonder we were pleased to be in a car with such powerful acceleration! On such things depended life —or death.

The night we set off to drive to our friends' house was pitch-dark. There was no moon, no light at all except the long beam of our headlamps. We had already travelled a considerable distance when suddenly the car started to drag ominously, as though caught in a patch of soft sand.

"What is it?" I asked anxiously.

Armand grunted. "Of all places to get a flat tyre!"

We slowed down and skidded to a standstill and clambered out to inspect the damage. The darkness

81

enveloped us like a cloak within its warm and secretive folds, while beyond its soft embrace there whispered the myriad sounds of the night.

At a time like this any commonplace noise could take upon itself a most sinister meaning. The shrill giggle of a hyena was no longer that sound which had so often stirred my heart around our house in Langata. We could no longer interpret it safely as the delighted voice of Africa awakening to the night, but rather, perhaps, as the high-pitched, mirthless cackle of a terrorist. Although we had a torch we scarcely dared use it for fear of attracting unwelcome attention, and for the same reason we switched off our headlights and did our best to see by the dim red light of our tail-lamps.

There were a spare tyre and jack in the boot of the car, but the jack was of an unusual type which we had never seen before. We inserted the lever at its base and started cranking. But nothing happened. The car did not rise a fraction of an inch.

"There is only one thing to do," said Armand, when it became obvious that our efforts were leading us nowhere. "Let's try to find a large stone by the side of the road and see if we can get the wheel off the ground by driving over it."

It was a long and laborious business, first to find the right kind of large stone in the darkness, and then slowly to drive over it accurately enough not to cause further damage to the car. But it was still no use. However much we pulled and struggled we were quite unable to remove the wheel.

At the best of times this would have been exasperating but in Mau Mau territory it was terribly dangerous.

Finally, when we had all but exhausted ourselves

through our fruitless efforts, I turned impatiently to Armand and said:

"I think one of us ought to start walking."

I remembered the occasion when Armand had once sprained his ankle and our car had broken down on a deserted stretch of road. Then I had to walk for days to fetch help. But quickly I put the thought from my mind. At least this road was not totally deserted. Sooner or later I was bound to arrive at a house or village, and even if it meant walking all night it would be infinitely preferable to waiting helplessly in an immobile car.

"As a matter of fact," said Armand, "I know of a house quite near here. It belongs to old man Vandy. Do you remember him?"

To be honest, I did not. I must have met him at a party or perhaps on safari soon after Armand and I had been married, but his name meant nothing to me.

"We can't leave the car unguarded all night. Goodness knows what would happen," said Armand.

"Well, I'll walk," I said.

Armand disagreed. If I were to stay in the car and lock all the doors, he argued, I would at least have some protection. But before he had even finished speaking I had already walked off into the darkness and he did not dare to raise his voice to call me back.

The black night totally engulfed me as I plodded on. Once I stumbled into a culvert at the side of the road and had to scramble out on my hands and knees. I smiled grimly to myself, for Armand had often teased me about my extraordinary ability to fall down holes, both in cities and in the wilds. He always said that if there were a single hole in a long street, I would be bound to get my heel stuck in it!

As I continued walking an almost irresistible desire to look behind came over me. Indeed, when once I did glance round I felt convinced that I had seen a menacing shape flitting from side to side of the road. I wanted to run, but with an effort of will managed to restrain myself. This was panic. I forced myself to turn around and stare into the darkness and even to walk back a few paces. It had been my imagination, of course. Suddenly the dark clouds had parted and revealed the shadows of the trees; they appeared to dance like animate beings for a split second before the clouds closed once again and blackness descended on the land. Chiding myself for having been afraid of shadows, I turned and continued on my way through the darkness.

Presently—it seemed an age—I saw a tiny light, like a pin-prick in a vast theatrical back-drop, shining straight ahead of me. For a moment I thought it might come from a Mau Mau encampment—though I very much doubted it, for the terrorists were far too expert bushmen to betray their whereabouts in such an obvious way.

I went on cautiously—until at last I arrived at the source of the light—a house within an enclosure surrounded by a barbed-wire fence about eight feet high. This, I guessed, was old man Vandy's property. I ran forward eagerly and tried to open the gate, but it was securely padlocked. No one seemed to be guarding it, so I called out at the top of my voice:

"Is anyone at home?"

There was no response, and had it not been for the fact that the house was fairly brightly lighted I would have thought it deserted.

I wondered what time it was, and glanced at my wristwatch. A quarter-past eleven. Perhaps everyone was asleep? But surely there would have been an *askari* or nightwatchman on duty?

I called again, louder than before. My voice sounded raucous in the darkness, even to my own ears, and seemed to awaken a response from my fellow-prowlers of the night. A hyrax* answered me, its voice sounding like a rusty watch being wound up to the full and then, on a different note, running down again. A baboon grunted as he was suddenly awakened in his roost and all his companions then started barking querulously at one another. They quietened down after a moment, however, but in spite of all the noise they had made there was still no sign of human life within the enclosure. Everyone, I reckoned, must be asleep, including the watchman. That did not surprise me, since my experience of most nightwatchmen had led me to suppose that they are extremely heavy sleepers whose habits were unfortunately diurnal rather than nocturnal. This impression, I hasten to say, may have been due to the fact that we had been employing a series of Juluo nightwatchmen, and the Juluo were inclined to be fond of *bhangi* or Indian hemp.

Becoming impatient, I decided to climb over the gate. But just as I was carefully negotiating the strand of barbed-wire which ran along the top of it, a rifle-shot, fired at almost point-blank range, crackled across the enclosure. The gate shuddered as the bullet struck it and I almost toppled over.

Had the place been taken by Mau Mau? I thought, in a panic.

Another shot rang out.

"Hi!" I yelled, with every breath in my body. "This

---

* The hyrax is a strange little animal, no more than eighteen inches long, yet remarkable for the fact that its nearest living relative is the elephant.

is Memsahib Denis!" But although I was badly frightened I was suddenly overcome by an idiotic desire to laugh, for it had dawned on me that whoever was shooting was obviously under the impression that I was a terrorist raider.

"This is Memsahib Denis!" I shouted again and, if possible, louder.

Mercifully the firing ceased, and as I clambered down from the gate I saw, emerging from the darkness, the figure of a white-haired old man, with a rifle. Behind him followed an African carrying a *panga*.

"Well, I'll be——!" exclaimed the old gentleman, peering towards me. "What are you doing out there by yourself? I could have killed you. We thought you were Mau Mau." Then, with sudden indignation, he demanded: "How dare you go wandering about by yourself, madam?"

"I beg your pardon," I replied. "I came to borrow a jack. . . ."

"A what?"

"A jack," I repeated. "My husband and I—our car broke down. It was a borrowed car and didn't have a proper jack. . . ."

The old man shook his head slowly from side to side and mopped his forehead. "I—I'm damned sorry, my dear," he muttered.

I glanced at him mischievously. "You nearly ruined my best shirt," I said, with mock reproach.

My remark made us both laugh—from relief, perhaps. I felt sorry for him. He was obviously one of the old school, and the realization that he might so easily have killed me appeared to be an even greater shock to him than it had been to me.

"Do please come in, my dear," he said, leading me

towards the veranda of his house, "and let me give you a glass of brandy."

I assured him, however, that I was quite all right and had no need for a glass of brandy, but added that I was rather worried about my husband. "He's out there all by himself with the car," I said. "If he heard those shots he's probably thinking——"

I checked myself, aghast at having aggravated the old man's already acute embarrassment.

"Oh, my God," he sighed, collapsing into one of the deck-chairs on the veranda. Hunched and pale faced, with his white hair haloed in the lamplight and his nicotine-stained moustaches drooping lugubriously like bunches of faded primroses, he presented a picture of utter dejection. "He probably thinks you are dead. . . ."

"Yes," I said, "it is quite possible. . . ."

"My God," he repeated, drawing a hand across his brow. "We must do something. . . ."

"I had better get back to him," I said. "If you've got a jack . . .?"

"Yes, I have a jack."

"Perhaps I could borrow it? I need a Tanganyika jack—not one of those new-fangled things which don't work."

I had said just the right thing. The old gentleman perked up and grunted agreement. "None of this would have happened if you'd had a decent jack," he growled. "It beats me why people have to go on inventing these useless new gadgets. Why can't they stick to the old reliable ones?" Grumbling to himself, he rose from his seat. "Of course, my dear," he said, patting me on the shoulder, "you can certainly borrow a jack—a proper, old-fashioned Tanganyika jack—with my sincerest compliments."

87

Limping slightly, he led the way to a truck which was parked at the back of the house and invited me to clamber into the front seat beside him. The gate was opened for us by his African boys, two of whom jumped aboard as we drove out and set off along the open road.

The distance which I had travelled on foot seemed astonishingly short by truck. Within a few minutes we caught sight of the dimly glowing sidelights of the car, and I could see Armand striding towards us with a formidable-looking branch, rather like a cudgel, grasped firmly in his hand. We pulled up as we drew level with him, and I jumped to the road.

"Not a scratch, you see," I cried.

He was tense, almost angry in his relief to see me. "What happened?" he asked.

"Don't speak about it now," I replied, in an undertone.

Old man Vandy had now recovered his composure at the sight of our reunion. "I hear you need a jack," he said, descending from the truck, and immediately set his boys to work changing our tyre.

"Did you hear gunfire?" asked Armand.

"A little," I replied, "but it was nothing to worry about. I did a silly thing, that's all. I tried to climb over a gate, and this gentleman mistook me for a Mau Mau. He did his duty and tried to stop me."

I left it at that, and in order to save the old gentleman's feelings I did not tell Armand what had really happened until several days later. And by that time we were already so deeply engrossed in our next assignment that this embarrassing little incident had been practically forgotten.

CHAPTER EIGHT

SIMBA KALI'S ESCAPADE

SIMBA KALI was beautiful in her cat-like way. She was neat, strong, elegant—and the size of a small greyhound. Simba Kali was a lynx or caracal. Her coat was beige with undertones of cream. Her small head was handsome, and on each dark ear, a pointed tuft stood erect. But as viewers of our television programme may remember, Simba Kali was a bundle of fire and fury, even when young.

She was born on Raymond Hook's farm at Nanyuki. Raymond had captured her parents who had borne several litters, and so Simba Kali had been semi-domesticated all her life.

Both Armand and I believe that if you have an animal when it is young and treat it with kindness, it will always respond, but our theory went wrong with Simba Kali. Either she came to us too late or she was quite untamable. Her incredible beauty tempted you —in the face of all your experience—to fondle her, but if you went too far, the dainty velvet claws struck with lightning speed and dug deeply into your flesh.

We all hoped that some day we would soften the hard heart of this beautiful wild cat. We would woo her and imagine that at last we had won her over to us. She would look so trustingly into your eyes. She would sit with her feet tucked neatly under her chest, like a domestic pussy. If you said flattering words in her ears, she would close her eyes demurely, acknowledging your homage. But if you tried to press the friendship further, teeth and claws would rebuff your advances.

But for a miracle Simba Kali one day would have blinded me. We were on our travels in the Somali desert country and had stopped at a remote spot so that we and our collection of pets could eat.

Food was prepared and we were sitting in the shade of the big truck when suddenly we heard chattering voices. A crowd of friendly Somali girls, tawny-skinned, oblique-eyed, in gaily coloured robes, gathered round us, looking at our equipment and the food we were eating in wide-eyed amazement.

"Look, look!"

Simba Kali, sitting on my lap, had caught their attention, and warily—though foolishly perhaps—I lifted her up so that the girls on the edge of the crowd could get a better view.

The moment I touched the cat, she slashed out at my face with her long, cruel claws. I felt a burning pain immediately under my eye and dropped the cat at once. Armand rushed over to examine my wound.

"A quarter of an inch to the right, and you would have lost your eye," he said gravely.

But in spite of Simba Kali's unpredictable moods, I could not help loving her and hoped one day that the cat would soften her heart and Armand would be able to show her on television as a reformed character.

As always, on this trip, we had had nothing but kindness from George Lowe of the Veterinary Department, and his wife Lois, and thanks to their introductions, hospitality was showered on us all the way through the Northern Frontier Department to the border.

At Garissa, the veterinary officer was going on safari and insisted on lending us his house. His boys brought us firewood and water, and a Somali from his staff was attached to us to smooth out any difficulties. We had travelled fast for many miles in difficult desert country and the time had come when we must thoroughly clean our equipment and begin work.

The surroundings were ideal for filming Simba Kali and we hoped to show her off in a more tractable mood. The cat had lately developed the habit of wandering off by herself and this was worrying; there were too many prowling hyenas who would make short work of her.

But here at Garissa there was no need to keep the cat on a lead. She could run at will in the enclosure which was ideal for filming. It was empty except for a single building—a small hut used by the Africans as a lavatory. The light was just right, there was nothing to distract our temperamental young star, and only me or Des on hand for her to bite. It seemed an ideal set-up.

A camp chair was brought out for me and we began. I coaxed Simba Kali on to my lap and Des started to direct me for his photographs.

"Now, if you'll just——" he began.

But before he could finish Simba Kali had dug her claws into my arm and spat in my face. I tried to keep my hold on her but this time she used her teeth and I had to let her go. She streaked away towards the hut and beyond.

Both Des and I were after her in a flash.

"Go *that* way," said Des, as he dashed round to the other side of the hut. We met on the far side, but Simba Kali had disappeared.

Des and I looked at one another and began to laugh. "It serves her right," we said in the same breath. We had both guessed what had happened. The cat had taken refuge in the little hut. But when we opened the door, there was no sign of her.

"Surely she couldn't have fallen down that hole!" I exclaimed, shuddering.

91

I will not go into details about that hut, nor will I enlarge on the indescribable smells that came up from the deep pit below. Unpleasant though the work would be, I knew what we had to do if Simba Kali was to be rescued.

But first we had to locate her. Des flashed a torch into the pit and we peered down at the sludge at the bottom. There was no sign of her. That, I felt was something— but where was she, then? Slowly we followed the beam of the torch as it swung round, and then, there she was, sitting on a narrow shelf in the wall of the shaft.

Miraculously she was unhurt, and when she saw us, true to her type, she spat angrily.

"We *must* get her out," I said, "if we don't, she'll starve or fall deeper into the pit. She can't get out without our help."

The floor of the hut was made of thick concrete, and we could not enlarge the hole without a great deal of trouble. As we considered the position, Des had an idea.

"Let's lower one of our fruit baskets at the end of a rope," he said.

A *kikapu*, as the basket is called in Swahili, was ideal for the job since it could be folded flat and pushed through the hole. We fixed one to a rope, squeezed it through the gap and lowered it, hoping the cat would have enough sense to jump into it. As an added bait, I put a piece of meat in the bottom of the basket.

For several minutes the basket dangled invitingly by the shelf, held in the beam of the torch. The cat watched our efforts without interest, sitting in her favourite position, with her feet tucked beneath her. She didn't even move, when to make things easy for her we managed to swing the basket right on to the ledge by her.

Finally, she yawned, stretched, and with a "why-don't-you-leave-me-alone?" look up at us, jumped down on to the caked residue at the bottom of the pit. Des manoeuvred the basket down to her just as Armand arrived and, looking faintly surprised, asked what we were doing. I put a finger up to warn him to keep silent and he joined us on his knees at the aperture in the floor.

Slowly, in absolute silence, the basket swung towards Simba Kali and as it touched her, she saw the meat. We held our breath while she tried without success to hook it out with her paw. Suddenly, in what seemed to be one effortless movement, she leaped into the basket, seized the meat, and was out on the other side before we could haul her up. I could have cried with disappointment.

It was now time for lunch and after a quick meal we began all over again. Our television deadline was close and we could not stay at Garissa any longer. If, in the next few hours, Simba Kali could not be persuaded to jump into the basket, she was doomed to a lingering and unpleasant death. For once we left, no one would trouble about a wild cat in a pit.

Simba Kali seemed as disinterested as before. Even another piece of meat failed to tempt her. Now, light was our difficulty. We had to keep a pencil beam on the basket to attract her attention to it, and manoeuvring both torch and basket through the narrow hole in the floor was no easy matter. Also, our supplies of torch batteries were not inexhaustible.

"If only we had a constant supply of light," said Des thoughtfully, wandering off in the direction of Queen Mary.

I continued to swing the basket, watched now by a small crowd whose comments on the conduct of two

Europeans in the *cho,* as they call the smallest room in Swahili, were not flattering.

"The Memsahib and Bwana have gone mad," said a Somali with conviction.

A moment later, he was quite sure. Des returned with a naval flare we had brought with us for experiments in night photography. "This is just the thing we need," he said. "It'll just go through the hole."

I felt doubtful about the wisdom of setting off a magnesium flare in the hole and went off to seek Armand's advice. "Disastrous," he said at once. "Des mustn't do it."

But it was too late. When we returned to the hut, the flare had already been dropped down the shaft and the fumes were beginning to rise. The smell was impossible. Smoke swirled and eddied upwards from the floor and with tears running down our cheeks, we all rushed out, coughing and choking. To add to the macabre effect, scores of enormous cockroaches staggered drunkenly from the shaft.

"That's the end of Simba Kali," said Armand in a death-bed voice.

Des looked stunned, for he was genuinely fond of the wayward animal. "I never thought this would happen," he murmured wretchedly.

At last the light of the flare died and the fumes stopped rising. We went into the hut again. An African offered us a small lamp, but alas, that was too big to push down the hole.

I picked up the torch again to see if I could locate Simba Kali's body. Silently the three of us tried to probe the murk. Des suddenly seized my arm.

"Good lord, there she is!"

Following the direction of his pointing finger, Armand and I could not believe our eyes. There she

94

was indeed, her paws tucked under her body, calm and collected, and gazing up at us.

"What an amazing thing!" Armand exclaimed. "I wouldn't have thought anything could have lived through those fumes. Simba Kali must be indestructible!"

We couldn't leave her to her fate after that, but what on earth were we to try next? The basket method was a failure.

"Why not make a loop and drop it over her body?" suggested one of the Africans. They were now as keen as we were to rescue her.

Armand shook his head. "Even if we could, she'd struggle all the way up and hang herself," he said.

It was getting late and we were all exhausted. Simba Kali would have to spend the night at least in the nauseous hole. We went to bed, but immediately after breakfast the next morning returned to the hut with a new scheme. The hole in the floor must be widened and Armand and Des begun wielding a pickaxe taken from the back of our Power Wagon.

"Whoever made this *cho* must have had a secret yearning to build military fortifications," said Armand, sweating, as he handed over the pickaxe to Des.

It was indeed a masterpiece, intended to last for ever. Under the first three or four inches of concrete, there were iron bars and the concrete then went down another eighteen inches.

At last the hole was widened to admit a man and Des began testing the strength of the rope we had been using to lower the basket.

"I'm going down," he announced.

"I'm the smallest," I protested.

"Nonsense," said Armand at once. "Let me go."

But Armand was the heaviest of us all, and after a

95

little more argument, Des had his way. He made a loop for his foot and put another loop around his waist as a safety line.

The question of the lingering fumes in the pit troubled Armand.

"If they affect you in the slightest degree, shout and we'll haul you back," he cautioned.

The Africans were now urged to come forward, and with Armand as their leader, took told of the rope. They were as excited as we were as they watched Des disappear into the blackness of the pit. Personally, I would rather have entered a burning building to rescue the cat than descend into that murky, loath-some mess.

It did not take long for Des to reach the bottom. He shouted to us that he was all right and asked us to lower a box on a rope.

"But, quickly!" he gasped. And we understood the need for haste.

The episode was almost over. Des grappled with Simba Kali, but game to the last, she tried her best to claw him. Seconds later, she was inside the box and in Des's arms and had been hauled up to the top, to the cheers of both the Africans and ourselves.

The smell they brought up with them was quite un-believable, and both were hurried to the bathroom at once. It did not improve Simba Kali's temper to be scoured, but in spite of her claws she had to submit.

After this adventure, we had had our fill of wild cat. When we returned home, we sent her back to Raymond Hook at Nanyuki. Simba Kali seemed none the worse for her harrowing experience and from time to time we hear news from Raymond of the fine family she is raising.

In the fabulous
Hadramaut of
southern Arabia

The author

CHAPTER NINE

A HAIR-DO—BY MAWINGO

OUR house at Langata often resembles a zoo. We have had as many as eighty-five animals in and around the house at one time. Many of our pets are allowed complete liberty, but those who are likely to be aggressive to other animals are always kept in large, strong enclosures. These enclosures are necessary for another reason. Wild leopards around Langata are a great menace, and every year scores of dogs and other pets are carried off. So it is as much to keep wild animals out as to keep our own pets in that we have built them.

Pets can lose you friends—and at the very least cause embarrassment. A Swiss couple we know kept a young rhinoceros, called Johnny, whose pleasure it was to pretend to ignore anyone who called. Then, when a small group of visitors stood chatting in the garden, young Johnny would lumber stealthily over and charge them. More than once I have suddenly felt the impact of a sharp horn, then Johnny's full weight, and next moment I would be sprawling on the lawn.

Somehow our hostess's reproof, "Yohnny! Oh, isn't Yohnny a naughty boy!" did not altogether console me for my bruises.

But animals, whether they are pets or not, are like people in many ways. You often think you know your friends, and are reasonably sure of their reaction to any given situation. But every now and then they do not react in the way you expect. Neither do animals.

Animals do not acquire a personality simply because

97

they come in contact with human beings. If you watch a group of wild animals you will soon discover that each one is quite definitely an individual. Once, for instance, we photographed an elephant who had the curious habit of throwing grass into the air so that it fell on to his head and back. As we watched, he seemed to be feeding quite normally. Then, suddenly, as he chewed and looked reflectively into space, he pulled up a trunkful of grass, and, instead of eating it, whisked it up over his head and shoulders.

We must have watched thousands of elephants, but neither Armand nor I had ever seen another one behave in this way. Armand had a theory. "I think he does it to keep the sun off," he said. But the next day, when the sun was not shining, the elephant behaved in exactly the same way. "It must be a habit," said Armand at last, "like a man biting his nails or scratching his nose."

Everyone knows pets will cling all their lives to a trick they learn when they are young, and that it is easy to teach them without employing cruel methods. When Bimbo our baboon was small, I taught him a simple trick. I used to hold my leg in my hands and say over and over again, "Poor Bimbo, poor Bimbo." Immediately, Bimbo began to copy my action. He staggered and hopped about on one foot, doing a very creditable imitation of a baboon who had suddenly been shot through the leg.

Bimbo became exceedingly proud of this trick and would always do it at any time visitors were around. The words, "Poor Bimbo!" would start the baboon running around holding his leg as if in excruciating pain. Often he would do this without being asked and was extremely pleased when our visitors laughed.

Arranging for the care of our pets when we are on safari is quite a problem and, as a rule, we leave many of them with our neighbours the Rootes—Alan and his young-looking mother. When Bimbo stayed with the Rootes, he was always kept on a very long chain near trees so that he could climb and jump from branch to branch. But he was both wily and resourceful and it needed a strong chain to hold him. He escaped many times, and the stories we were told on our return of his escapades were long and terrible to hear.

One day after he had managed to free himself, Bimbo made for the nearby *duka*. Before the owner of the *duka* could grab him, Bimbo was leaping from shelf to shelf, leaving behind him a trail of scattered and damaged goods. A bottle of whisky attracted him—he examined it with great interest, all the time keeping a watchful eye on the anguished proprietor. Finding he could not open the bottle, he hurled it with great deliberation on to the cement floor. The exploding bottle startled the baboon even more than anybody else and with a great bound, he leaped through the door and went running up the road into the bush.

It was some time before Alan Roote discovered that Bimbo was missing, but he soon tracked him to the *duka*, which looked as if it had been swept by a tornado.

"He went that way," said the owner.

Alan paid for the havoc and walked on up the road, unhopefully calling as he went, and searching the bush on either side. A car approached in a cloud of dust and he was hailed by the driver, who stopped and got out. It was a European, obviously pretty shaken.

"I say, old man," he said, "is . . . is that your baboon up the road?"

Alan said it no doubt was. He explained the baboon had escaped and he was looking for him. The driver looked even more guilty.

"I'm terribly sorry," he said, "I'm afraid I must have hit him. He's up there hopping about the road on one leg. I could have sworn I cleared him by a good four yards . . . can't understand it." He stared in amazement as Alan burst out laughing, and dashed off up the road, calling back, "Do wait a moment!"

Alan returned a few minutes later with Bimbo in his arms.

"The rascal!" he said, and went on to explain Bimbo's trick. It was a very relieved driver who got back into his car and drove off.

Bimbo had been in our zoo, mateless, for some time, when a friend gave us a large female baboon whose name was Mawingo. Would Bimbo take her as his wife? When she arrived we put her in her own cage, as it is never wise to put animals, even of the same species, together until the ground for friendship has been carefully prepared.

The first day Mawingo was rather shy, but the day after, she seemed to have recovered her spirits, and I decided to make friends with her myself. I stood by her cage and began to make loud smacking noises with my lips in the way baboons do. Mawingo gave me her paw to groom and I parted the thick fur with my fingers, making friendly noises all the time.

When you groom a baboon, you do not look for fleas, which in any case are only to be found on sick monkeys, but for small flakes of skin which contain salt. Grooming makes all monkeys ecstatic, and when baboons groom each other it is a sign of trust and friendship—also courtship.

Still smacking my lips I groomed the back of

Mawingo's small strong forearm and prepared to leave her. Mawingo at once opened her eyes and made loud smacking noises back. We were friends.

I hadn't gone a step away from the cage when Mawingo's arm shot out through the bars and she grabbed my hair. The shock made me wince, but it was no time for panic, and I stood quite still while she groomed my hair enthusiastically. Becoming more and more affectionate she pulled me right against the cage, jerking my head and neck into a thoroughly uncomfortable position.

This can't last long, I thought desperately, she'll soon get tired of it. But two, three, four minutes passed, and she showed no signs of tiring. I decided to take action. Reaching for her forearm, I tried to groom her again. But she wasn't deceived. She pushed my hand away, and holding my hair more firmly than ever, went on grooming me lovingly.

I was now in a thoroughly awkward predicament. Baboons are obstinate creatures, and I knew that Mawingo would hold on to my hair even if I tried to free myself by force. To have a fistful of hair torn out by the roots was too agonizing to think about. And another thing: I had no wish to destroy the friendship I had successfully started with her. Mawingo was in any case fully grown, with an impressive set of teeth, and if she misconstrued any action of mine she certainly wouldn't hesitate to bite. I would have to wait until she tired of the game, or until someone came and rescued me.

I do not know how long this well-meant grooming had gone on, when Mwangi, our African contractor, appeared at the door of the main house—but it seemed a century. He did not at first see me, and I was terrified he would go away.

"Mwangi," I called.

At once he turned, and hurried towards me. Mawingo grunted forbiddingly.

"Stay where you are, Mwangi," I said. The baboon had lowered her pale eyelids over her golden brown eyes and I felt her hand tighten on my hair. Her inch-long teeth flashed. She was prepared to defend this new friendship to the last. Baboons are notorious for their quick tempers, and I was determined to keep Mawingo in a good humour as long as possible.

"Go and tell *Bwana Yangu* (my master) to come here at once," I said in a low voice.

Minutes passed and Armand did not come. Mwangi, who was both intelligent and alert, I knew could be relied on to give Armand my message. I wondered despairingly whether Armand had gone out or could not be found.

By this time Mawingo had moved farther up the wire mesh and in doing so had stretched my neck as far as it could go. She had begun to groom the side of my head farthest from the wire, and I felt as if my neck would snap at any moment. The pain was so intense that I thought at last I must sacrifice my hair and make my escape. I eased away from the baboon slightly to see whether it was possible to get away unscathed, but Mawingo's reaction was immediate. Red-hot needles seemed to have been thrust into my scalp and she pulled me so hard I thought I should be drawn through the wire mesh.

Tears of pain sprang into my eyes and in my agony I could have screamed. But I remembered to make the friendly noises and Mawingo responded by grooming my hair more enthusiastically still. I could see my watch and had counted every second of ten minutes when I heard the door open. Through it I could see

Kundukubi our cook and Tshikadi our other boy, walking down the kitchen steps towards me.

Help was at hand at last, but the problem of how to use it still remained. If the boys came too near the cage, Mawingo was certain to fly into a temper, and even though I freed myself I knew I should suffer dreadfully in the process. Then I had an inspiration.

"Bring some bananas," I shouted hoarsely.

The boys realized the situation was desperate, and were up the outside stairs of the house almost before I had finished speaking. A moment later Tshikadi advanced towards the cage carrying a large bunch of bananas. Mawingo still clung to my hair and watched the proceedings, suspiciously.

"Take them to the far end of the cage," I whispered.

The manoeuvre succeeded. As soon as she saw the bananas lying on the floor, Mawingo let me go and grabbed them. I all but collapsed, and for a moment thought I should lose consciousness. I closed my eyes tightly in an effort to compose myself, and opened them moments later feeling better, to see the boys looking at me anxiously.

Rubbing my head, I began to see the funny side. I smiled, and the boys grinned back uncertainly. They had been wondering whether to laugh or not, and now, seeing me unhurt, they suddenly burst out laughing. I could not help joining in, in spite of my sore and aching head.

"Memsahib looked so funny, held prisoner by the baboon!" roared Kundukubi, with tears in his eyes.

As soon as we had enjoyed this doubtful joke, I went to find Armand. He was in the cutting room deep in conversation with Des about a piece of intricate apparatus which stood on a bench before them. They did not move as I entered, and I had to repeat Armand's name twice before he looked up. The manner of both men made it all too clear I was interrupting important work.

"What is it, Michaela?" asked Armand.

I controlled my feelings with difficulty. "Didn't Mwangi ask you to come outside about half an hour ago?" I asked.

Armand looked at me blankly. "Good lord, yes! So he did," he said. "Well, what is it you want to show me? An insect you've caught? A bird? Can't you show me later—you can see we're busy."

I told them, somewhat haughtily, what had happened. They laughed.

"It's the story of the little boy who cried wolf," he said. Then he apologized for not responding to my S O S, although he could not resist adding, "But I hope it will teach you a lesson, Michaela."

CHAPTER TEN

CHIMPS AND CHEETAHS

EVERY pet we have kept has its own distinct personality: whether mischievous or sedate, humorous or sullen, spiteful or good-tempered. Even among the same species animals are complete individuals.

Our two chimpanzees, for example, are entirely different. Emily, who came from England, is unpredictable and at times ferocious, while Pickle, who joined the household from America, is a lovable little clown, who adores to be noticed and petted.

Chimpanzees do not live naturally in Kenya. Their habitat is the Congo, though very properly they enjoy protection from hunters. If the regulations were lax, a black market in chimpanzees might easily spring up. Happily, the rules are enforced rigorously all over Africa. Consequently it is very hard indeed for people in Kenya to acquire a chimpanzee.

Emily, then, was flown out to us from England, and we were waiting at Eastleigh airport, at Nairobi, when she arrived. Her box was lifted gently to the ground and she looked out at us quizzically. She was much bigger than we expected. As I looked at her, she poked out one long brown finger and touched my hand tentatively. A crowd had gathered, and everyone wanted to talk to her, but we thought she would be frightened, and quickly put her in the jeep, and drove off.

We were taking Emily to the Rootes, as we were due to go on safari in a day or two and wanted to avoid upsetting her by too many changes. When we arrived, we let her out of her box and she stood on the soil of Africa for the first time. Born in Europe, she had returned to the land of her ancestors. She lifted up her arms, inviting Armand and me to take one each.

"Hang on to her," Armand cautioned, "she may panic and run away. It's all new to her, don't forget."

But Emily had no intention of running away. She hung on to us firmly as we walked her round the grounds to give her the feel of her new home. Bimbo had already been moved to the Rootes' home, and was soon aware that a newcomer had arrived. Alternately he threatened and enticed the chimpanzee and Emily, on her part, showed interest too. But Armand restrained her. "I don't think it's wise to let them get together tonight," he said.

Emily was not easily persuaded, however. We managed to get her away, but every now and then she decided it would be amusing to go to Bimbo's box and talk to him. After some difficulty we at last managed to divert her attention and walk her over to the house.

Tea was ready and we entered the kitchen to reach the drawing-room where the meal was set out. Two African boys gaped when they saw Emily padding along with us. They had never set eyes on a chimpanzee before and did not seem to like what they saw. They fled in panic but soon returned, and looking through the door laughed delightedly at the strange new animal.

Emily had been on her best behaviour in the garden and we decided that she could be trusted to run loose in the drawing-room. She was obviously pleased to be free and freedom made her bolder. She showed an interest in everything in the room and took a particular fancy to a small coffee table which from time to time she beat like a drum.

"Emily would probably like some tea," Armand suggested when we had begun.

A milky tea was mixed and sweetened and Emily thrust forward her lip to its fullest extent to let a little trickle on to her tongue. Then she drank the whole cupful and smacked her lips with pleasure, plunging her fingers into the bottom of the cup to get the remains of the sugar.

"How adorable she is," commented Mrs Roote, watching her lick her long fingers. Emily seemed perfectly at home. She let Mrs Roote cuddle her. Satisfied that she was in good hands and would settle down, we drove home to finish our packing for the safari.

Next morning Armand drove over with a snake, which the Rootes had promised to care for during our absence.

"I shan't be long. Be ready for the road the moment I come back," he said.

Everything was packed, so I locked up the house and put on my ex-army jacket to wait for Armand's return. The sun rose higher in the sky and still there was no sign of him.

I passed the time watching a fawn and brown lizard on a wall at the back of the house. It was quite invisible when it kept still, but in movement—as when a fly came near—it changed into a lightning flash of quicksilver. Another lizard came creeping up, trying to poach on this hunting-ground, only to be chased off in an instant. The lizard in possession nonchalantly chewed the flies he had caught—and that reminded me of something. I was hungry. Whatever time could it be, then? Startled, I realized it was past midday, What had happened to Armand?

I wondered whether to drive over to the Rootes' house at Karen, but decided against it. I might as well eat something though. So I unlocked the house and made some lunch, washed up and locked up again. Still no sign of Armand. Ought I to go in search of him? I was thinking of doing this when he drove up.

He seemed exhausted and clearly put out, but we were so late that he insisted we should start out straight away. As we reached the road he said gloomily, "Emily practically destroyed the Rootes' house last night."

"*Emily!*" I repeated stupidly. "Did she break out of her sleeping box, then?"

"They couldn't even get her *into* the box," Armand replied wearily. "She wouldn't move from the living room. She bit Alan when he tried to take her out. So the Rootes thought the journey might have upset her and let her sleep in the room. She was quiet when they left her, but the next morning—you should have seen the mess! Lamps broken, cushions torn, even the window frames smashed."

"Oh, how frightful for them," I said in dismay. "But I expect you put her into an enclosure when you got there?"

Armand shot me a testy glance. "The Rootes and I have been having a pitched battle with Emily all morning and afternoon. With just a break for lunch." I judged it wiser to say nothing, and eventually Armand went on, "We finally got her box to the door of the kitchen, and put some food in to entice her. In the end we had to capture her in a net and bundle her in. She fought like a demented tiger."

After that momentous battle we could never give Emily the freedom we would have liked. But Pickle was different. He arrived a few weeks later, ten months old, about the same size as a human baby of the same age and needing exactly the same care. In intelligence, however, he was a little more advanced than a ten-month-old baby.

"It's sad, isn't it?" said Armand, after we had been playing with Pickle one day, "in six months' time the great gulf between man and the anthropoids will have been reached."

I nodded. A human child of the same age as Pickle would then begin to speak, but Pickle would never learn. He showed great ingenuity in using tools and perhaps would draw after a fashion, but he would never be able to tell you even what he had for breakfast. In a human child, the glorious process of growing and developing would begin but Pickle would grow only in size.

But while he was a baby, Pickle played just like one. It was not long before he could hold his own cup of milky tea and drink it by himself. Like many human babies, he liked to finish by up-ending the cup on the top of his head. He knew it made us laugh and he laughed with us, showing his little teeth. If he was tickled, he made a funny little gurgling noise and held his sides in helpless laughter. The Africans loved him and many of them came from the other side of Langata to see him.

I have kept many cheetahs as pets. But one in particular I shall never forget.

We went to take pictures on Mount Kenya and it was a wonderful experience. We drove up the narrow track past forests of great trees festooned with ghostly, greenish-grey Spanish moss, through a belt of swirling mist, and into the pale sunlight beyond. The track ended and we continued on foot between what looked like trees but were actually giant lobelia and ground-sel. In this eerie world, we felt like Lilliputians. When we finished our work we descended to Nanyuki, where

I decided to buy a thick woollen scarf which could be wrapped over my head to keep out the biting wind.

Nanyuki is not a large place—merely a wide street with *dukas* and petrol pumps on each side. The *dukas* were well stocked with scarves, but none were woollen. We went from shop to shop trying to find one thick enough. Trucks were parked along the street, and as we passed one of them, Armand stopped. The vehicle which had attracted Armand's attention was different from the others. In its expanded metal body were two unusual passengers: a full-grown cheetah and an Alsatian bitch.

They made a handsome pair, the cheetah with its small head, and spots and black lines from the inner corner of the eye to the outer corner of the mouth, and the Alsatian with dove-grey fur that was long and silky. We tried to stroke the cheetah through the mesh of the cage, but the Alsatian jealously pushed him out of the way. He, on the other hand, docilely allowed the bitch to be caressed. It was intriguing to see a domesticated animal dominating a wild one.

I went off again in search of a scarf, and when I returned, Armand was talking to the owner of the animals, a Welshman named Jones. His camp was not far away and he readily agreed to allow us to photograph his animals out of their cage. "They play like kittens together," he assured us.

It had been raining before we arrived at the camp and the animals had been kept in, but Jones was willing to let them out before night fell.

"Aren't you afraid of losing them when you let them out?" Armand asked curiously. We both knew that cheetahs have a habit of gazing into space, and suddenly darting away in search of something their keen eyes have spotted in the far distance.

Jones laughed. "This fixes them," he said, holding up a leg of lamb. "I always feed them at this time. No matter how interested they are in their game, they always come back for their meal." He added that the two animals were fed together, and when Armand asked whether the dog was allowed to eat a little of the cheetah's meat, Jones laughed.

"Is the *cheetah* allowed to eat the *dog's* meat, you mean," he laughed. "That bitch is a proper terror. He has to wait until she's finished. Then he eats what she leaves."

The animals were let out and they ran in circles, leaping and gambolling like lambs. Unfortunately the location of the camp made it useless for taking photographs, and in addition, the grass in which the animals were playing was far too long. We discussed the problem of finding a suitable place and finally arranged to go to the race-course on the following afternoon.

Jones was waiting when we called and the animals were loaded into the truck. Alongside him in the driver's seat was a parcel of an unusual shape. "It's their dinner," he explained. "With animals, you never know! Do you?"

The race-course appeared to be deserted, and with his assistant's help, Armand set up the cameras. "I do hope they'll play in strange surroundings," I said. I needn't have worried. They did play, romping like kittens, and Armand soon had a fine series of pictures. But as we watched, entranced, the cheetah suddenly, and without warning, stopped playing. With body tensed it looked into the distance. It stayed like this for perhaps ten seconds. Then, swift as an arrow, it was gone, leaving all of us, including the Alsatian, utterly astonished.

As the cheetah is the fastest animal on earth, attaining the speed of sixty miles an hour, it had covered some distance before we started after it. It seemed to be heading for a field on the far side of the race-course, in which a game of polo was being played. As we panted up, we were greeted with cheers from the spectators, and to our horror there was the cheetah, right in the middle of the game, alternately chasing the ball and stalking the horses and their riders from one side of the field to the other. The expressions of the players varied from indignation to incredulity.

If Jones had not arrived just then, jumping out of the truck, which he had brought to the edge of the field, and brandishing his leg of mutton—all the while calling to his cheetah in heart-rending tones, a very ugly situation might have developed. For a moment we wondered whether the leg of mutton would prove more attractive than a nice fresh horse, but the manoeuvre succeeded. Slowly the cheetah was coaxed near the open door of the cage. The Alsatian which had never left her master's side, was ordered to jump in, the mutton was thrown in, and the cheetah followed.

Thankfully we slammed the door on the cage and turned to face the polo players, as they came jogging up. They were extremely good about it, and stayed on to watch the two animals feeding together.

The cheetah's temper, as he waited his turn with the leg of mutton, was still ruffled by the excitement and he spat and slashed out with his front paws, when anyone came too near the cage.

You may have guessed the end of this little story, but I will put it on record. Yes, the cheetah was very much an individual, and we managed to persuade his owner to sell him to us. We felt we could cope with any trouble he might get into. We bought the Alsatian, too, for we could not bear the thought of parting the two friends, and they are still living happily together in their own enclosure, and when we can supervise them, outside as well.

CHAPTER ELEVEN

"GIN FLING"

JAMES BONNINGER, a friend in the Department of Information at Machakos, south-east of Nairobi, had told us about some magnificent drumming and dancing he had witnessed in his district. Several times he had implored us to film it, and had even offered to arrange a performance especially for our benefit. He spoke of it with such infectious enthusiasm that we drove to Machakos and installed ourselves as guests for the night in James's house.

Early the next morning Armand, Des, James, and I set off into the wilds. The drumming, James said, took place in extremely sparsely populated country, so sightseers would not worry us. We drove all day and arrived at our destination, which happened also to be an encampment for Mau Mau prisoners, at sundown.

In a little hut just outside the barbed-wire perimeter a young man in khaki came forward to greet us, looking rather surprised to see a white woman among the arrivals. He was the District Officer—tall, blond, blue-eyed, and incredibly youthful in appearance—whose name was Norman. Ordinarily, Norman's tough job would have been undertaken by an older and much more experienced man, but the troubles were at their height and he was out there on his own.

I looked with curiosity at the uniforms of the prisoners inside the cage. They were wearing white shirts and loose-fitting white jumpers. Some of them had one broad black stripe across the chest, others had two, presumably to distinguish the bad from the very bad. We had brought no servants with us, for the good reason that we did not wish our boys to risk contamination with convicted Mau Mau, so we were allocated two elderly Africans to work as houseboy and cook. One of them had a single black stripe on his shirt, the other two. They appeared affable enough and willingly set to work preparing a meal with the provisions we had bought at a *duka* in Machakos. In the meantime, we motored the seventeen-odd miles to the village where the drumming and dancing were to take place.

The little village itself was a joy to behold—a cluster of mud and wattle huts with attractively thatched roofs. The chief was extremely pleasant, plump, placid, and most accommodating. We told him that we were not interested in anything which was not entirely African, and he was good enough to give us his word that his dancers and drummers would be wearing nothing but native dress when they staged a special performance for us on the following day. Delighted by this assurance, we bade him a temporary farewell and drove back towards Machakos, stopping *en route* to call at a small Italian Catholic Mission which was quite close to our camp. One of the missionaries, who professed a great interest in ethnography, appeared to be so fascinated by the ways of the African that we decided to invite him to go with us to the dancing. In my heart, I was hoping that the things he would see would not be forbidden by his religious organization; but I reassured myself with the thought that Catholic missionaries are usually far more broad-minded and intelligent than those of many other faiths. We made an appointment to pick him up in the morning, and then we returned to the camp.

Before dinner I went to the kitchens to see how our Mau Mau recruits were getting on with the cooking.

We started talking, and I found them to be two delight-ful old Kikuyus whose evident liking for me was en-tirely reciprocated. God knows why they had ever agreed to take the Mau Mau oaths, but I felt that it must have been through intimidation. Nevertheless, it was a strange and rather disturbing sensation to know that one of our domestic helps had vowed to kill every European he could find and the other had promised to steal everything he could lay his hands on.

"We would very much like to stay and work for you, memsahib," said the elder of the two, after we had been chatting for an hour or more. He then solemnly gave me both his and companion's name and address for future reference. What splendid credentials, I thought, for domestic service!

After dinner that evening I wandered across to the wire-encircled compound to have a chat with the sentry who was standing there beside an old-fashioned brazier of the type used by nightwatchmen in my childhood.

Within a short time several men had gathered around us, and I noticed with some surprise that several of them were prisoners. We talked of many things—of people and places, of food and cultivation, of drumming and dancing, but never, of course, about the crisis in Kenya. With as little movement as possible I made quite sure that none of the prisoners was stand-ing behind me, for one could never tell whether a man had been pressed into Mau Mau service against his will or whether he was a fanatic—a potential killer. When dealing with large and dangerous wild animals which have ostensibly been tamed, it has always been a policy of mine to keep them in full view and never give them a chance of creeping up behind me. It was the same with these Mau Mau prisoners. The risk of something going wrong may have been small, but I saw no reason to take it unnecessarily. At all events, everything went smoothly and I very much enjoyed our conversation. It was quite an experience. The prisoners behaved perfectly, evidently enjoying the opportunity of talking with someone from the outside world, and when finally I left them they begged me to return the next day to continue our chat.

It was early morning when we set off, having packed a picnic luncheon. James and Norman were accompanying us, and on our way our party was augmented by the inclusion of the Catholic Father, whom we picked up at the Mission.

We were not long in reaching the dancing ground, where we found a vast crowd already gathered, swaying and stamping to the intoxicating rhythm of a host of drums. Attached to their biceps the drummers wore large ostrich plumes which rose, billowed, and fell like the flow of surf upon the shore. We were enchanted by what we saw and heard, and delighted that James Bonninger's enthusiasm had been so amply warranted; but we had been spectators of this thrilling performance for no more than half an hour when our pleasure was suddenly dampened by the sight of an Army jeep pulling up beside us.

"We heard there was a dance on," called one of the officers. "Any objections to us taking some pictures as well?"

Of course, there was no question of our having any objection, for after all these were the men who were keeping law and order in the land.

"By all means, go ahead," replied Armand. Then he turned to me and whispered: "How did they know there was a dance on?"

"This is Africa," I replied. "Forgotten? Everything is known, sometimes before it even happens."

The words were barely out of my mouth before a second jeep arrived. This time it was the Police.

"Hi, Bill!" called one of them to an occupant of the first jeep. "We heard there was a dance on." Looking round, he noticed Armand and Des, whose cameras were already set up for action. "Mind if we take some pictures?"

Armand shrugged. He looked miserable.

"Go ahead," he replied.

A somewhat florid, square-faced individual then left the group of policemen and came towards us. He was of medium height and supported a tyre of fat around his waist which was blatantly premature in a man who could not have been more than thirty years of age.

"My name's Bendorpt, Public Relations," he announced. "Do you mind if I watch you filming?"

He seemed inoffensive and friendly enough, so we did not actively discourage him. So long as he kept quiet and did not get in the way while we were working we could scarcely object.

Soon we were getting some wonderful shots, the film was building up fast, and the cameras were already being reloaded. During this brief respite I noticed some old ladies grouped together who looked as though they were itching to dance. I started to shake my shoulders at them, in imitation of the other dancers, and they immediately made a circle around me and we all danced together. Heaven only knew when they had last performed these intricate steps, but obviously they were thrilled to dance again. Chuckling and displaying their toothless gums, they wriggled and shuffled with all the abandon of young girls. These capers had not been long in progress, however, when over the sea of bobbing heads I saw that Armand was looking for me, so I excused myself from the circle and joined him.

"Time for lunch," he said, pointing to his wrist-watch.

I rounded up the rest of our party and we went across to the tree beneath which we had left our box of provisions.

But as we approached it we were horrified to see Bendorpt lying blissfully against the tree-trunk with a bottle of gin—our gin—tilted to his lips at an angle which clearly showed that it was practically empty. A bottle of vermouth, moreover, with the cork removed, was lying beside him. I picked it up and turned it upside down. There was not a drop left. Those two bottles had been our entire supply of liquor for the trip.

"Do you mean to say you've finished off *all* this yourself?" demanded Armand, his voice controlled but angry.

A hiccup answered him.

The South African staggered to his feet and, without a single word, lurched away before we had recovered ourselves.

"You've swilled our three days' rations like a pig!" I called after his retreating figure. But already he had vanished into the crowd.

Luncheon was a rather dull affair without our usual aperitif, but we soon forgot our loss when we got back to work. We were greatly helped by the Catholic missionary, who seemed to be everywhere at once, offering advice and encouraging everyone.

The excitement mounted and we were scarcely able to keep pace with events. On the one hand, a long line of drummers, like some undulating and befeathered centipede, beat out a rhythm of increasing intensity. On the other, a group of male and female dancers shimmied and postured with their noses pressed one against the other—a style of dancing which reminded us forcibly of scenes which we had witnessed and photographed in New Guinea, but which we had never previously seen in Africa.

The men, holding their drums upright with their right hands, maintained a rhythmic beat with short wooden sticks while swaying in front of their partners. Simultaneously, the girls executed the sensuous motions of the dance with absolutely expressionless faces which added to the calculated seductiveness of their movements. The old ladies, meanwhile, were still shuffling around in a dance of their own, and when they saw me approaching they gleefully beckoned me to join them. I was on the point of doing so, but at that moment Des called me aside.

"Our South African friend," he said, "wants to sleep with the chief's daughter." His serious young face looked even more earnest than usual.

"That's terrible," I exclaimed. We could not afford to have trouble with these dancers who were staunch Mau Mau haters. But trouble there would be if Bendorpt molested the girl, and I felt how unfair it would be for the dancers to suffer for what they might do to him.

Des left his camera where it was and together we went to warn the rest of the party of this alarming turn of events. It was necessary to exercise the utmost caution, for the large Mau Mau camp was not very far away, and as news travels fast in Africa we had to conceal at all costs the fact that white men were quarrelling among themselves.

Eventually we found Bendorpt sprawling under a tree with three African belles giggling around him. Before he saw us coming he staggered to his feet and grabbed one of the girls around the waist. She gave a delighted little squeal, but before the affair could go any further we marched over in a body and broke the party up. Bendorpt protested energetically, but we were firm, and the girls went running back to join the dancing.

As we made our way back to the arena, James Bonninger remarked:

"I heard the police say they would take him back to his camp."

A police jeep arrived some ten minutes later and we sighed with relief to see what we hoped was the last of Bendorpt.

We worked until nightfall. We had collected a mass of material and enjoyed ourselves enormously, and finally waved our friends goodbye and clambered into our trucks with the feeling that we had spent a thoroughly rewarding day.

After dropping the Italian Father at his Mission, we drove along the winding road to our camp, and with the help of our two Mau Mau assistants, soon prepared a make-shift dinner. Our gin and vermouth had gone, and as a substitute I could produce nothing more appetizing to drink than cooking sherry. But even before we had a chance to sit down and taste that, a police jeep drove up and our friends of the morning hailed us.

"Hullo there!" called one of them. "Just thought we'd check up on our South African acquaintance. He was pretty far gone when we last saw him."

"But didn't you take him with you?"

"No, he said he was going with you."

"Nothing of the sort."

"You mean he isn't here?"

"Of course not."

"Oh, my God!"

Norman's large blue eyes nearly popped out of his head and he went quite pale.

"This is terrible," he muttered.

"It certainly is," agreed one of the policemen. "We're on duty tonight and can't waste our time chasing after a drunk."

"So we'd better go and fetch him," suggested Des.

"I'll go with you," said Norman. "You'll need some help."

I said: "I want to go, too."

"No," said Armand, "you stay here. Two are quite enough."

"But maybe I could persuade him to come without trouble," I protested.

"Don't worry about that," said Des, clenching his fist. "We'll persuade him all right."

I begged them to let me go. "We can't let the Africans see us quarrelling amongst ourselves. If we can persuade him quietly it would be much better. From what I've seen of him he's probably more likely to listen to a woman."

My point was taken, so I was allowed to go with them. But as we were short of petrol for the return journey, we decided to travel in Norman's small car.

Driving along in the dark was a frightening business, for the thick bush on either side would have afforded perfect cover for any band of Mau Mau desperadoes. Each corner held danger, for we were never to know as we turned if a tree-trunk would be lying across the road. Presently we drove over a little wooden bridge and knew we were passing close to the Catholic Mission. There was always water in the rivulet beneath, but at this time of year it was usually fairly shallow.

We drove as fast as possible, for it seemed to us that

every minute we were on the road mischief might be done which could not later be undone. However much Bendorpt deserved a knife in his ribs, the tribe would be bound to suffer if anything like that happened to him. Besides, for a European to be involved in a sordid affair with an African woman would be an appalling blow to the white man's prestige, especially at such a critical time.

"He kept saying he was going to have the chief's daughter," said Norman. "I told him not to be such a fool and that we'd all be in danger if he did." He gave a deep sigh. "Oh, why did this have to happen while Med was on leave?" Med, I guessed, was his District Commissioner.

Although we had to travel only a short distance our journey seemed interminable, but finally we heard the throbbing of drums and saw a glow of fires against the night sky. Was it our imagination, or had the drumming a wilder quality about it—something almost threatening?

We pulled up at the village and jumped out of the car.

"Where is the *musungu*?" demanded Norman, in a voice which was high-pitched and tense. "Where is the white man?"

"He is over there," said a native, pointing into the darkness.

We followed his direction but found no sign of Bendorpt, and although we searched frantically in the darkness and asked several other natives if they had seen him, he still eluded us. But then, suddenly, we heard his thick voice shouting:

"Come here! Come here, you little bitch!"

Quickly we ran in the direction of the voice and found the man a moment later. He was crawling on all

123

fours in pursuit of a high-breasted young girl whom he was trying to grab by the legs.

Norman rushed forward. "Get up!" he commanded. "On your feet!"

The drunken man looked up with an expression of fury and annoyance.

"I'll do as I please," he grunted with an oath. But at that moment Des bent down and yanked him to his feet. Bendorpt swayed before us, placing his legs wider apart in order to try to balance himself. While Des grasped him by one arm Norman took hold of the other, and together they started to lead him towards the car. He was so surprised at our sudden appearance that his drink-sodden brain did not for a time register the fact that he was being guided towards the vehicle. But as soon as he saw the car he broke away from his escort and took a few steps backward.

"I'm going to stay here with my friends," he announced. "You can all keep your hands off me!"

"I'd better clock him on the jaw," muttered Des.

I stopped him. "Let me try a bit of persuasion," I said.

Bendorpt turned his back on us and started staggering away, and I must admit that had it not been for the thought that the Africans would be blamed for any harm that came to him I would have abandoned him there and then. However, it was obvious from the angry looks of several men around us that they would soon be provoked beyond endurance, and that what had started as a carefree revel might end in a nightmare of murder.

"Mr Bendorpt," I called, running after him and slipping my arm through his. "Mr Bendorpt, my husband and I would so much like you to come and have dinner with us."

I could not help smiling a little to myself at the formality of this invitation.

He paid little attention to me and continued on his unsteady course.

"I can't come tonight," he said, staring straight ahead. "I've promised to dance here. Perhaps I'll come tomorrow."

"But we shall be going tomorrow," I protested, suddenly glib. "You must come tonight. We were so kindly entertained when we were in South Africa. Please allow us to extend our hospitality . . ."

I had managed by sheer force to arrest his progress and somehow succeeded in manoeuvring him towards the car.

"Please," I said. "You can come back after dinner to join your friends."

"Will you bring me back?" he demanded.

"Yes, yes, after we've had dinner."

He was in a dangerous mood and I knew that if I was to persuade him to come I would have to humour him.

"Come along," I entreated, "the food will be getting cold."

The doors of the car were already open and I pushed him into the front seat beside Des, slammed the door, and jumped into the back with Norman. We set off without a moment's delay.

If the journey out had been difficult, the return journey was infinitely worse. Bendorpt had suddenly decided, as drunken people will, that he had made a friend in me, and it was all I could do to prevent him clambering over the back of his seat to join me. Once he lurched against the steering wheel, causing the car to swerve dangerously, and on another occasion he squeezed my hand so violently that I felt my wedding-ring cut into my finger.

As we passed the Catholic Mission we heard the sound of drums and singing, and I remembered that the Italian Father had mentioned that some of his young boys were being circumcised that night. The Mission had not been established long in the district and the Father considered that the circumcisions should be performed there, rather than in the villages, hoping that the boys might return in later years and become candidates for conversion. This was a normal Catholic means of forging a link between the natives and the Mission, and it was an important occasion. However, the fact that we were passing the Mission meant something far more important to us: we had only half a mile farther to travel.

At last we stopped outside our bungalow, ushered Bendorpt out of the car and sat him in a chair on the veranda.

Armand, tired after the long day's work, had already eaten and gone to bed, so I went to the kitchen with Norman and James to see about some food for the rest of us. A moment later, however, we heard angry noises from Armand's bedroom. I raced inside and was astonished to see him frog-marching Bendorpt out of our room. Grasping the unwelcome visitor by the scruff of the neck and the seat of the pants, he threw him out, slammed the door, and went back to bed without a word. Breathing heavily, Bendorpt subsided in an arm-chair and stared moodily about him. I made no comment, but hastened to produce some plates of soup which I set on the table, and we all sat down to eat without further ado, for by this time we were very hungry. All of us, that is to say, except Bendorpt, who eyed his plate with evident distaste.

"Did you see what that fellow did to me?" he grunted, glowering at each of us in turn. "He threw me out. I don't think I care for that. I've been in some of the best messes in the country and it's never happened to me before. Yes, I've been in some of the very best messes."

When he found that he could extract no response from us, he jutted out his chin. "I said I'd been in some of the very best messes in the country. The Police Mess, the P.W.D. Mess, the Sergeants' Mess, the lot! And this has never happened to me before."

He shook his head, then fixed his gaze on me. He was looking for allies.

I suggested he should eat. He took a couple of spoonfuls of soup, then pushed the plate away.

"Did you see what that fellow did?" he repeated.

It amused me to hear Armand referred to as "that fellow", but Bendorpt's monologue was obviously also intended for my husband's ears. It was raucous and defiant.

Suddenly he sat up and said: "I'm going back to the dance."

He tried to stand up, but I quickly pushed him back in his seat.

"Wait a moment," I said, and rushed out to the kitchen to fetch more food. Des came with me.

"Now I wish I had knocked him out," he said. "There'll still be trouble."

"Think what wonderful propaganda it would have made for the Mau Mau if we'd been seen fighting amongst ourselves," I said. An idea struck me. "I tell you what—let's make him drunk. Maybe he'll pass out."

"Drunk on what?" asked Des.

"Cooking sherry."

When we returned to the veranda we were just in time to prevent Bendorpt from getting to his feet again, and it was obvious now that we would have to take drastic measures to hold him.

"Here, drink this," I said, handing him a large tumbler of sherry. "It'll do you good."

He drained the glass at a gulp, but for all the effect it had it might as well have been a glass of water.

Our "cellar" was now empty and I watched Bendorpt hopefully, imagining that the cooking sherry would have a delayed effect. But no; he was still articulate.

"Now I'm really going," he said, levering himself out of his chair and taking a few paces out of the bungalow. We were too quick for him. We all jumped up and forcibly pushed him inside again.

"You really must stay for coffee," I said. "Or, as your hostess, I shall be most hurt."

Bendorpt's monologue continued and once more he got up. Again we pushed him down. Norman by this time was in despair. I signalled him quietly to join me outside.

"Haven't you a dispensary?" I asked him when we were out of earshot.

He nodded. "Yes."

"If you've got a dispensary it shouldn't be difficult to quieten him," I told Norman. "There must be a mild anaesthetic which would put him to sleep . . ."

At that moment James joined us. "I think he ought to be clapped in gaol for the night," he said. "If he gets among the natives again he might endanger the lives of every European in the district."

I agreed with James, but Norman would not hear of it.

"We can't lock up a European with all these Mau Mau around," he protested. "Think how it would look."

128

Armand gazes from Uganda to the Congo

Zebras and lions—part of Africa's magic

"It would look good," I said. "It would show that we're impartial. If people don't behave properly they should be treated alike, whatever colour they are."

But Norman could only look woefully dejected.

"Don't worry," I told him. "This could have happened to anyone." I suggested we should go across to the dispensary, so we went out into the darkness and groped our way to the hut of the African Medical Officer. I explained in Swahili that we wanted a sedative—nothing dangerous or lethal, merely an effective sleeping draught. The man nodded and disappeared for a few moments. When he returned he brought with him an innocuous-looking brew in a medicine glass, and handed it to me with the assurance that it would induce a deep sleep without any after-effects.

On our way back to the bungalow I wondered how we could get Bendorpt to take the draught. In his coffee, perhaps? But when we reached the veranda we realized that the problem had solved itself.

Bendorpt had vanished.

He had pretended to fall asleep, and Des, thinking he could be safely left alone, had gone to reload the cameras and clean the equipment. Now the bird had flown—though how he hoped to walk seventeen miles in pitch darkness to the dancing place was beyond comprehension.

"There's no point in going after him now," I said. "We'd never find him on a night like this. He's probably too drunk even to keep to the track."

"Let's hope he's passed out in a ditch somewhere."

With these words we all went to bed and next morning told the Bendorpt story to the Italian father, who joined us for breakfast.

"I suppose we'd better go out with a tracker and try to find him," said James.

The missionary smiled. "No need for that," he said with evident enjoyment. "I can tell you what happened."

We looked at him amazed.

"Last night," he went on in his quiet voice, "we were down by the river during the circumcision rites. Suddenly we heard a sudden splash and then a shout. Some of the boys scrambled down and fished a man out of the river—he'd evidently missed the bridge and fallen head first into the water. I recognized your man Bendorpt at once. As we carried him to the Mission he kept saying, 'Well, I knew I could do it—I walked that seventeen miles pretty fast.' He had evidently heard our dancing and singing and thought he was back at the dance place!"

We shouted with laughter at this, and the missionary went on, "We managed to put him to bed. And whether he was over-awed at the thought of spending the night in a Mission, or whether his ducking had cooled him off I don't know, but he didn't move for the rest of the night."

"Where is he now?" I asked.

"He's outside. An army truck stopped at the Mission half an hour ago, and we asked them to take him back to wherever he came from."

We went out to have a last glimpse of our reluctant guest. He looked shocking. Blue-chinned, with bedraggled hair and crumpled rough-dried clothes, a coating of greenish slime on his shoes, all his bravado had gone. He looked crestfallen and sullen. We did not speak to him, nor he to us. A few minutes later he was driven away and we never saw him again.

As Armand remarked, "He should never have been in Public Relations. He belongs in a public house!"

CHAPTER TWELVE

THE ELEMENT I FEAR

I HAVE so often been asked by people who are interested in our work if there is anything I am afraid of. Well, there is. Water frightens me.

One day I hope to conquer this fear. But at the moment, whenever we undertake an assignment which involves working on river, lake, or sea, I am always assailed by a feeling of apprehension. Once we are actually on the job, my fear leaves me—but I suppose that applies to every form of fear. I have found that if you persevere and keep busy you never have time to be afraid.

One of the most alarming experiences I have ever had took place on a day when there was no hint that we might become involved in any danger whatsoever. We had been invited by our friend, Dr Louis Leakey of the Coryndon Museum in Nairobi, to go with him to Rusinga Island on Lake Victoria, where he had recently discovered a site rich in palaeontological treasures which even included insects and seeds many thousands of years old. For some reason I cannot remember, his wife, Mary, who is also a palaeontologist of great repute, was not with us on this occasion. Perhaps it was the time she flew back to England with one of their most exciting discoveries—the skull of a prehistoric forerunner of man. So fragile was it, having involved days of painstaking work to piece together, that she had nursed it on her lap all the way from Nairobi to London for fear that it might fall into fragments again.

We started off early one morning, accompanied by Bernard Wicksteed, the well-known British journalist who is now, alas, dead. Bernard was a modest, unassuming man, who radiated a quiet dependability. You always felt that you could rely on him for both sympathy and understanding, and it must have been this quality, shining through all his work, which made his reputation. He often came to Africa on assignments, and he always looked so English with his pipe and his old tweed coat.

The conversation between Bernard, Louis, and Armand was so entertaining that our long journey to Kisumu seemed to be over almost before it had started. Leakey made his subjects glow with interest, and with his Nordic good looks one could easily imagine his forbears in the costume of the ancient Vikings.

Having bought supplies at Kisumu we drove out to Louis's boat, which was a motor-launch with a single cabin and an outer deck covered by a sort of awning. As soon as the food and baggage had been packed on board we set off across the placid, mirror-like surface of Lake Victoria.

Louis's African assistants were waiting on the shore to greet us when we reached the island. He appreciated their work and told us how rapidly they had learned to sift the earth they dug and extract from it whatever was scientifically valuable.

The island was so rich in specimens that many of them had actually been found on the earth's surface, but there was nevertheless a great deal of digging and sifting to be done. I was so excited that I had scarcely been able to sleep in anticipation of the morning's work. Although I had once accompanied an archaeological expedition in South America—a most memorable event in my life—I had never been on a palaeontological excursion before. There is something truly awe-inspiring at the thought of discovering something of great antiquity. It gives one a sense of balance and values, and underlines the futility of worrying about one's personal problems. The evidences of life which we were about to unearth could have been reckoned in millions of years, while our own—that is to say, man—measured only a few hundred thousands.

On this day Louis was especially anxious to find specimens of seeds and insects, and both Armand and I were greatly flattered at being allowed to help. Crawling on hands and knees, I sieved industriously and was delighted when I discovered several small round objects of uniform size. "Seeds," I thought to myself, and I glowed with pride.

"Have you found anything, Michaela?" called Armand presently.

"Wait till you see what I've got," I replied.

"You mean you've really found something?" he asked, incredulously.

"I certainly do."

But alas, my pride was soon deflated. When I bore my specimens in triumph for Louis's inspection, he picked one of them up in his fingers and beckoned me to come closer. There was a twinkle of high amusement in his eye.

"Michaela," he said, holding the minute round sphere before me, "don't you recognize goat's dung when you see it?"

I was chastened. But a prehistoric goat, maybe? Decidedly not! It was strictly twentieth century.

I heard Armand chuckling behind me and felt myself blushing. After that I was much more cautious in what I presented for inspection, but even so I still solemnly brought Louis Leakey another piece of goat's dung before the day was out. However, I was also suc-cessful in unearthing two seeds, and of this discovery I was as proud as though I had found the skull of a Neanderthal man!

On the following day I had a real find. With the little trowel I had borrowed I unearthed the socket of a bone which had obviously belonged to some enormous animal. I did not disturb it, for I was well aware that archaeological and palaeontological discoveries were often made worthless because no exact data concerning strata and positions was available. Excitedly I called to Louis, who immediately came over with some of his assistants and proceeded to extract my find from the earth which perhaps had surrounded it for aeons.

It was a single bone—and nothing more. I was dis-appointed, because I had secretly been hoping that we might have discovered an entire skeleton. Louis identi-fied it as the femur of a prehistoric rhinoceros, and gave it to me as a present.

Later, in spite of Armand's vigilant eye, I managed to take this trophy by air in my suitcase to New York, and it was not until we were packing to go to New Guinea and Australia that he finally discovered it.

"What have you got in your suitcase?" he demanded.

"Nothing, nothing," I replied, and quickly changed the subject. "What time is our plane leaving?"

But I must have looked guilty.

He unlocked my suitcase and, ignoring my wails of protest, removed my precious bone from its hiding place beneath a set of nylon undies. Thus, instead of travelling with us, it was left in storage in New York. But I hope one day to have it sent to our home in Kenya.

Both Armand and I could happily have spent many months on the little island on Lake Victoria, but we all had to go back for various reasons—Louis to his museum, Bernard to England, and Armand and I to carry out our next assignment, which was to film some native drumming and dances. Very carefully Louis packed all his latest discoveries and stored them aboard the launch. All his African assistants lined up along the shore as we were leaving and waved us farewell with sad and solemn faces.

Lake Victoria lay blue and unruffled, as smooth as a highly polished floor. It became quite warm, and we went on deck and lay under the tarpaulin awning. There we talked of many things — of books and palaeontology—and I made Armand tell us about the lives and habits of gorillas, about which he probably knows more than any other person in the world. We listened to him with such fascination that we scarcely noticed that it had started raining, and were startled to see raindrops the size of halfpennies thudding on to the deck, while the boat was beginning to rock. Soon the torpid surface of the water had splintered into thousands of white-crested waves, the sky had darkened, and a howling wind tore at every beam and timber of our little craft.

We crowded into the cabin as the rain came down in torrents. The waves were increasing in size with alarming rapidity, and the vessel quivered and creaked in protest like a living being. There was a crash as a row of glasses fell from a shelf and shattered on the floor of the cabin. Then a particularly large wave struck us, and swamped the boat from stem to stern. We started to bale as fast as we could while Louis and his African boatman took turns at the wheel. They heaved and struggled to keep the bows at right angles to the waves, but to our dismay the steering did not respond. It was clear that we were slowly being pulled round, and as soon as we found ourselves broadside on to the waves there was no doubt we would be capsized. I knew nothing about boats, but I could guess that much. Soaked to the skin, we continued baling like creatures possessed.

At times the screw of the boat rode right out of the water and we could hear it whirring impotently above the waves. Louis rushed to the stern. He only stayed there a moment, clutching the rail, but quickly came hurrying back, his face tensed and his blue eyes wide and startled. He was looking more like a Viking than ever.

"Quick, give me a knife," he shouted, just managing to make himself heard above the thunder of the waves.

We found a knife. He grasped it, and at once rushed on deck through the swinging door. I watched him as he struggled again to the stern of the boat and started cutting at the ropes which held the tarpaulin. One by one they snapped, and left the tarpaulin free to flap madly in the howling wind. Then suddenly, it had gone—carried away like a kite in a hurricane until it disappeared into the black sky.

With water streaming down his clothes, Louis made his way back to the cabin.

"That tarpaulin," he said, standing drenched in the doorway, "it was acting as a sail. We should be all right now, it's gone . . ."

In the nick of time he had seen what was happening, and had saved us from capsizing into that boiling water. We should have stood little chance if that had happened, for the lake was swarming with crocodiles. Only recently a boat carrying Mau Mau prisoners across to the other side had capsized and the crocodiles had made short work of both guards and prisoners.

The storm had blown up suddenly, and just as sud-

136

denly it subsided. The relief was almost an anti-climax and we flopped down into chairs, almost too limp to move. Armand squeezed my hand and gave me a reassuring smile. He knew I could not swim in those days—then he remembered that we had some chocolate in our baggage and found it.

As we all sat around munching it, we discussed our adventure, and then started to talk about the fear some people had of water. I had to admit it was my only phobia. Bernard listened sympathetically.

"To tell you the truth," he said, sucking at his pipe, "I wasn't too happy myself."

CHAPTER THIRTEEN

SNAKES I HAVE KNOWN

I DO not mind snakes. Many people, when I mention this, ask with a shudder how I can possibly handle them. Naturally I like to know where they are, for it is always unnerving to come across a deadly snake unexpectedly, but once I recover from the shock of an unrehearsed face-to-face meeting, I usually know how to react.

As pets, of course, they have limitations. Although I do not mind snakes I am not an addict in the same way that some people are in Africa, and the largest number I have ever kept at one time is eight. But I know that my snakes, in time, always recognize me. Once they learn that you are not going to try to kill them every time you pick them up, they are quite capable of showing pleasure at being handled. This is particularly true when they are caught young, and I know one woman who trained her pet snake to slide over her shoulder and drop into her lap whenever she gave tea parties.

I was once bitten by a nine-foot python when Armand and I were on safari in Kenya. Nature writes its own matchless scenarios in Africa and we had no special plans in mind that morning, except to look out for what was unusual or beautiful or perhaps droll.

Suddenly a cry went up that a snake was lying in the grass by the roadside, and looking where Armand pointed, I saw a python. From its condition I should think it had recently sloughed its skin (some Africans, incidentally, are so frightened of snakes that they will not touch even a sloughed skin). Normally before a snake sloughs, its colour becomes dull, its eyes glaze over, and it is generally lethargic. This was a beautifully marked specimen, which we decided at once to catch.

There is an art in catching a python. One thing you must never do is to get in front of it or the python will bite and then wrap itself round your body and squeeze you to death.

The python's tail was nearest Armand and he seized it. "Get the head, Michaela," he shouted.

I moved along its wriggling length, intending to grab it from behind, but before I could do so the snake had whipped round like a big skipping rope, with Armand holding desperately on to its tail.

"Look out!" shouted Armand.

The python, as it turned and twisted, saw me, and before I could jump out of the way sank its inward-facing teeth into my leg. The bite was not serious, but it felt as if a dozen small red-hot needles had been thrust into my flesh. I do not know what would have happened, if Armand had been forced to let go, or if the snake had followed up its advantage, but neither happened, and a second later I had skipped to one side and grasped the python behind its head. I could see and feel the ribs expanding and contracting rapidly along its length as it wriggled like a giant eel, but now we had it trapped and soon it was in the bag.

The python was a fat handsome specimen and I kept it for a long time in a big wire cage. Normally this species eats small mammals such as rats, though in farming country they sometimes take a sheep and have been known to eat children. But Farouk, as I called my python, was not very ferocious and became quite a pet, even if I did not altogether like his odour of dirty washing. I took the greatest care when I handled him, but once his initial fears were over, he would snuggle closely to me and I could tell that he thoroughly enjoyed feeling the heat of my body. I was really sorry that, when the time came to go on safari, Farouk had to be given away.

Some people think that snakes will attack human beings without provocation, but that is not so. It may be true of the three most dangerous and aggressive snakes in the world—the African mamba, the Indian hamadryad, and the South American fer-de-lance—but our great friend Baron Gaston de Witte, the Belgian herpetologist, always says that snakes are not aggressive unless they are mating or raising a family. Gaston should know. For this man with the high forehead of a scientist, grey-blue eyes, and jutting underlip, collects both flora and fauna for the great Parc National Albert in the Belgian Congo, and probably knows more about African snakes than any man alive.

While we were sitting on the balcony of his house at Rwindi Camp—a camp which, incidentally, blends impeccably with the African landscape and has all modern conveniences as well—Gaston told us the story of the snake that chased him.

He had let it be known that he was interested in buying a black mamba, and one morning a young African arrived with a vicious-looking specimen six feet long, held more or less securely by a forked stick.

"Very lively snake, Bwana," said the African who was obviously controlling his fear of it only by thinking of the price he could get. They began to bargain, and Gaston agreed to buy the mamba. He then tried to chloroform it. The snake was certainly lively, and before Gaston completed the operation the enraged creature managed to wriggle free.

140

The boy was out of sight in a flash, for he knew that a mamba can move at the speed of a galloping horse. Baulked of one target, the snake turned its attention to Gaston. "I was up the path and in my laboratory, with the door shut, at the speed of lightning," said Gaston. In spite of the chloroform, the mamba raced after Gaston, and he slammed the door only just in time. But the snake had not finished.

Between the solid door and the concrete floor of the laboratory was a tiny gap of no more than an inch, but the hissing mamba nevertheless tried desperately to squeeze through to reach his enemy. Fearing that it would succeed, Gaston leaped on to a table and scrambled through the window. Pausing for a moment only to pick up a stick, he raced round the building and with a swift blow killed the fighting mamba just as it was preparing to strike his terrified laboratory assistant.

Gaston has become philosophic about his experiences with snakes. Walking among the rocks at a village in Katanga in the Belgian Congo, he caught sight of the tail of a snake. Not more than twelve inches was showing, the rest of the body was hidden under a rock. Our friend did not recognize the snake, and thinking it must be a small one, took hold of the tail and began to pull.

"I pulled for quite a time and the more I pulled, the more there seemed to be left," said Gaston.

At length the head appeared, and to his horror Gaston saw that the snake was a black mamba! Fortunately Gaston was not unprepared, and he and his assistant, acting as one man, seized the snake before it could strike. The next moment, the bewildered reptile was in Gaston's capacious bag. In his laboratory, Gaston chloroformed the snake and measured it. The mamba was exactly six feet long—one of the longest Gaston had ever seen.

"It shows that with snakes you should always be able to finish what you start," says Gaston.

In our ordinary life we do not often see snakes, and they were certainly not in my thoughts when the Africans began to burn the grass. The burning of the grass is a centuries-old custom of African cultivation, always taking place before the rains are due. The skies become leaden, and the whole countryside is filled with smoke-haze and takes on the appearance of the coat of a mangy dog.

We had been on safari for some months, and having let our house, had taken a white cottage at a small hotel near Nairobi. It was an enchanting cottage with a thatched roof and a flower border and we also had a bathroom outside the cottage itself. After our long safari, I had a busy washing day, and it was luxury indeed to be able to turn a tap to get hot water instead of having to ask a boy to boil up water on a fire every time I needed it. What added to my pleasure was the temporary possession of a neighbour's cat, Lolli. He was most affectionate, and during my washing activities he was usually with me, talking to me in his sonorous Siamese voice.

There was one more shirt to wash. I went into the bathroom and was preparing to soak it in water when I heard three small bangs in quick succession at my feet. "Ha, ha," I thought, "it's Lolli, swishing his tail against the side of the bath." I bent down to stroke him, but saw, with more than a little surprise, not Lolli but a large snake wriggling along the bathroom floor. It was a miracle that I had not stepped on it and my heart missed a beat at the thought.

As silently as I could, I backed out of the bathroom

and walked quickly back to the cottage. Armand was reading in a chair.

"There's a snake in the bathroom, Armand," I said, as casually as I could.

He showed no surprise. "What kind?" he asked.

"I think it's a spitting cobra."

"Really?" said Armand in matter-of-fact tones. "I'd better have a look."

He was back a few seconds later. "It *is* a spitting cobra, quite definitely," he said. "It has just spat at me."

I knew a little about spitting cobras. I knew for instance that when cobras spit at a human being they always try to aim for the eyes. I knew too that they have an astonishingly accurate aim. Cobra venom injected by biting nearly always proves fatal, and even when spat out, it usually blinds a victim for three or four days.

Armand wiped the venom from his spectacles and together we set out for the bathroom.

"There'll be a panic if the news gets round that we've a snake in the bathroom," he said. "Or," he added, "if the snake tries someone else's bathroom."

Armand opened the bathroom door quietly and we peeped in. Outside the sun was shining and the green curtains filtering the light gave the room an eerie, under-the-sea look. The snake, curled up, was still there, but as soon as it heard us it slid obligingly into the adjoining lavatory. Armand jumped forward at once and closed the door on it.

"We'd better call in Johnny Leakey," said Armand.

Young Johnny, son of our friend Dr Louis Leakey, was a snake addict. He collected snakes and kept them in a large round enclosure as a hobby, and though his pets had bitten him once or twice, he had not lost his fondness for them. If Johnny could capture the snake alive, we knew he would be pleased at getting another pet and we should be rid of an unwelcome visitor. At the hotel we gave the bad news of the snake's presence to Norman, the owner, who resignedly shrugged his shoulders. "I am always afraid of this sort of thing during the burning of the grass," he said. But he added rapidly, "Don't tell anyone else. Some people might get nervous."

To my intense relief, Mary Leakey raised no objection to her son trying to capture the snake, but while we waited for Johnny to arrive, I began to feel uneasy.

"I've a presentiment, Armand," I said, "the snake is going to disappear."

Armand laughed at my fears. "It can't," he said, "unless of course it decides to go for a swim!"

Johnny arrived, equipped with a butterfly net, sacks and a box. He was thrilled and confident and walked straight into the bathroom without a tremor. We stood closely behind him as he moved towards the second door. He straightened his tall slim back and flung the door open. There was no sign of the snake. Johnny looked behind the curtains and behind the door. The room was the smallest and there was no other place where the snake could hide. Johnny looked back at us with a bewildered gesture.

"This is unreasonable, Johnny," said Armand. "The snake *was* here. We both saw it and the door has not been opened since."

We all crowded into the room and Armand looked at one or two tiny holes in the plywood walls.

"A cobra could not possibly have got through there," said Armand, pointing with his foot at one of the holes.

144

The new-born camel Armand wouldn't let me adopt
Cheetah, strangely enough, is my favourite cheetah's name

Jock Druett

These are not children with Armand but full-grown pigmy matrons

Pay as you earn, pigmy style

Amboselli's famous rhino Gertie emerges from the undergrowth

These Boran women show me how they weave watertight vessels

These Zulu twins became my firm friends

"It was far too big." He tapped the hole and the wood crumbled at his touch. White ants had eaten the wood away from outside and had left little more than a thin layer of paint.

"It *could* get through there," said Johnny with conviction. "A cobra as thick as your arm can wriggle anywhere."

Closing the door again we went back to the hotel owner and gave him the news. "It must be between the plywood and the weather-board outside," said Norman. "We simply cannot leave it there. Get a crowbar and break the wall down."

By this time the news had spread that we were hunting a spitting cobra and several guests gathered round our bathroom to watch. I stood outside with a stick to prevent the snake emerging into the open and Johnny and Armand went inside again, to break down the wall.

In a few minutes, there was a four-inch hole in the plywood and Johnny peered in cautiously. Anticlimax! The snake was not there.

"Could it have got on to the roof and escaped?" I asked Norman.

"Absolutely impossible," he said at once. "The roof is solid. The snake simply could not have got up there."

The only thing left was to start on the second wall, and after a few vigorous jabs, Johnny gave an excited shout.

The cobra came out, spitting right and left, and full of fight. I was outside and could not see what was going on, but in next to no time Johnny was hooting joyfully. He had secured the snake in his net and in a few dexterous movements had transferred it to the large box he had brought with him. When I went inside, the bathroom floor was wet with venom. I would never have believed, if I had not seen it, that the cobra could have spat so many times.

We all patted Johnny on the back as he triumphantly took the snake home. As far as I know it is still living in Johnny's enclosure.

CHAPTER FOURTEEN

THE CHARMER'S CHARMER

Now and then in Africa one hears of snake-charmers, and the rumours always make me eager to see them at work.

After one of our expeditions to make a series of films on pigmies, Armand thought it would be a good idea to show by contrast the Watusi, the giants of Ruanda-Urandi on the border of the Belgian Congo, reputed to be the tallest people in Africa. We had made several expeditions before to see the Watusi, but unhappily it always seemed to us that the giants were shorter every time we went back. Armand put this down possibly to a revolution in diet. In the old days the Watusi lived chiefly on milk and blood, and this had now changed. The Watusi now eat the same sort of food as everybody else in Africa. But worse than the loss of inches was the fact that the Watusi were slavishly copying the dress and ways of the white man. It was truly heart-breaking to find that most of them looked completely ordinary in shabby European-style clothes. The Watusi toga was a pleasing garment and gave the wearer immense dignity, but only one old man we met was still wearing it.

Years before, Armand had acted as technical adviser when MGM made the film "King Solomon's Mines" in the Watusi country. No expense was spared and, on Armand's advice, the film company went to the trouble of finding the old man who had designed the king's original royal hut. He was commissioned to construct a replica of the hut and with the good-will and co-

operation of Georges Sandrart, the local administrat
a wonderful structure was erected.

The venerable old architect was tall and look
kingly himself and two upstanding scrolls of hair on
head added to his height at least another eight inch
His hairstyle emphasized his thin, fine features, t
characteristic high cheek-bones and the slanting ey
at the same time it deflected attention from the son
what protruding teeth which are a national char
teristic of the Watusi. We were all thrilled to see t
royal hut grow under the skill and guidance of the
architect. He remembered where every post of t
original hut had stood and walked happily about t
site, giving instructions and gesturing with his lo
slim hands.

After the film was finished, Armand suggested
MGM that the royal hut be presented to the Watusi
a national museum. "A fine gesture," I said when t
news was made known. "This is a good day for t
Watusi."

I spoke to one of the officials who gave me a curic
look.

"You may think they will be proud of it," he sa
"but we know we shall have to put a guard on it or th
will burn it down."

Both Armand and I could not believe such a thi
would happen.

"Yes," said the official thoughtfully. "They h
their past. All the Watusi want to do is to imitate
slavishly."

"But it would be vandalism to burn down such
beautiful hut," I said. The official merely nodded
head and turned away.

So now, ten years later, we were back in the Wat
country, determined to find out whether the offici

words had been prophetic. We well knew the hillside where the hut had been built, but we walked over it several times before we would admit the awful truth to ourselves; the hut, constructed with such care under the direction of the old man, had vanished.

Searching around, we found the pitiful remains—three small circles of concrete which had been used instead of baked mud as a platform for the king's throne. I thought compassionately of the old man whose masterpiece had gone. Did he live to see the day the hut was destroyed? And what of the Watusi who had gone berserk and done the deed? Why, when they had so much to be proud of in their past, did the giants hate it? There was no one on the hillside to give an answer to my questions, and we turned and went sadly down the hillside.

Mutara, king of the Watusi, whom we saw at his palace next morning, was quite the tallest man I have ever seen. He would have looked more regal still if he had worn his toga, but alas! he wore European clothes for our audience.

He spoke good French and had been abroad to Belgium where, dressed in his robes, he had been a great success. I ventured to ask the king why he did not wear his own colourful robes at home.

"Oh, one must be modern," he said airily.

I had taken with me as a present a copy of my book *Leopard in my Lap,* but as I had not been able to find a French edition, it was in English. When I apologized to the king, he said: "That is quite all right. I shall learn English in order to read your book. There is an American missionary here."

The White Father at the king's side hitched up his long white gown and stroked his beard. "*We* will teach you English," he said hurriedly to the king.

We were anxious to meet the Queen Mother, and King Mutara arranged a visit for us on the following day. The Queen Mother's palace was built of brick; but inside, though there was plenty of evidence of European influence, there were also many objects of traditional African design such as carpets, basket wear, and various richly embroidered covers.

"The Watusi were always great craftsmen," said one of the Queen's household when I commented on the complicated elongated designs.

A single glance at Mutara's mother showed us that we were in the presence of a Queen. Armand is tall but the Queen Mother was taller. Her bone structure was fine and classical and she had the wise and indestructible beauty of the old. We talked to her through an interpreter; it did not take us long to realize that the Queen Mother was both intelligent and witty. More than once, I glimpsed a merry twinkle in her eye as she answered our questions and I thought it made her look astonishingly youthful. Before we left the palace, we were given permission to take photographs of the Queen Mother and her entourage, which pleased us greatly. But we knew we were still short of material for the programme on the Watusi we had set out to make.

The matter was on our minds as we sipped drinks in the hotel lounge that evening, and we were discussing the problem at length when a man at the next table leaned over.

"Forgive me for eavesdropping," he said, "but may I make a suggestion? Why not photograph the snake-charmers?"

At once we were all ears. "Where can we find snake-charmers?" we both asked together.

Our neighbour waved his hands in a circular motion.

"Oh, anywhere," he said blandly. "There are many snake-charmers. The Bahutu are quite famous for it, and so are the Watusi."

We knew that Bahutu was the name of the normal-sized race which lived in Ruanda-Urundi with the Watusi. From the earliest times the Bahutu have been the servants of the Watusi. The situation is still the same today, and it is not unusual to see a tall Watusi on a bicycle, flanked by two Bahutu boys who sprint behind as he pedals along. When the lanky Watusi comes to a hill, the Bahutu boys push from behind to make sure that their master does not exert himself unduly.

"Both Watusi and Bahutu are snake-charmers?" we asked our neighbour.

"Yes, both tribes." The Belgian's large, protruding eyes closed to emphasize his remarks, and then popped wide open again. "The snake-charmers will make a marvellous set of pictures. Yes," said the Belgian, banging the table. "What an easy life you have. Why, it's a holiday all the time! I only wish I could do it."

My eye caught Armand's and we smiled. It was no use explaining to the Belgian that we worked seven days a week for long stretches at a time. True, we loved our work and would not exchange our life for any other, but it did not alter the fact that often at the end of a day we were so tired that we fell asleep over our dinner. Apart from the physical exhaustion of long journeys there was the mental strain involved. All our programmes are planned ahead, and we have a dead-line to meet just like the newspapers. The fear that we might not have completed a programme when it is due is with us all the time.

"Well," said Armand, "our life is not all plain sailing, you know. Most of our time is spent looking for

151

things we don't find and that's what costs the money and takes the time. But these snake-charmers now, where do you think we can find them?"

The Belgian sipped his beer. "I have heard of one very famous snake-charmer. I've forgotten her name, but she lives about seventy miles from here."

Armand made a note of the name of the village.

"Of course you don't have to go that distance," said the Belgian. "Just walk out of this hotel and ask anyone —ask the first person you meet. He will tell you where to find a snake-charmer in the next village."

When the man had gone, I suggested we could do worse than adopt his suggestion. "All right," said Armand, dubiously.

The first person we met was a White Father. He was a small man with an enormous sun helmet which almost totally eclipsed the upper part of his face, and his thin greyish beard straggled from his chin on to his chest.

"Excuse me, mon Père." I told him we were making pictures for television and would like to photograph one of the famous snake-charmers of Ruanda. "Where can we find one?" I asked.

"Snake-charmers?"

The sun helmet tilted upwards to reveal two piercing and lively eyes. I had asked a squirrel in priest's clothing. He would certainly know. I felt nothing would escape such lively eyes.

"Snake-charmers?" repeated the little man. "There are no snake-charmers here. No, absolutely none. None at all."

I suggested that possibly he might not have heard of them. "Have you been here very long?" I asked.

"No, not very long, it's true. But still, even in twenty years . . ."

I gasped at the under-statement and thanked the father. Armand chuckled, and that chuckle made me determined to find a snake-charmer even if there was only one in all Ruanda.

"Let us ask the Africans, Armand. Maybe the Church frowns on snake-charmers," I said.

We walked arm in arm across the street and went into a shop crowded with Africans. An African was serving.

"I hope he speaks Swahili," I said. "You had better try him in French first."

Armand addressed the man behind the counter, and asked if he spoke French. When the African said he did, Armand explained our quest, and the African nodded several times.

"Yes, yes, yes," he said when Armand had finished. He turned his back, reached up to a shelf and produced a cardboard box.

"Here, here, sir."

We looked at the box blankly, until we saw the label: "Snake-bite kit." We shook our heads, and I explained all over again in Swahili that we had not been bitten. "We want to find a snake-charmer," I said.

"Ah, yes," said our obliging young man, "in Uganda there are ladies who charm the snakes."

"But we're not in Uganda. We want to find a Watusi snake-charmer."

"I will ask," said the young man. He translated what I had said, and from the amount of noise that ensued from his customers, it was obvious that there were two schools of thought on the subject of snake-charmers. There were those who thought there were no snake-charmers in Ruanda-Urundi and those who thought there were.

The shopkeeper kindly translated one or two of the comments for me.

"This man has lived here all his life and has never heard of a snake-charmer."

"This man's grandfather remembers that there were snake-charmers."

"This man says that in the nearest village is a snake-charmer. He is certain."

We ignored the negative school and concentrated on the man who said there was a snake-charmer living near his village. With the help of our interpreter we found out—more or less—where the village was.

We then walked to the next *duka,* which was empty, and asked the jovial proprietor where we could find a snake-charmer.

"Snake-charmers?" said the proprietor, when we had explained why we were looking for them. "What should they charm—we have no snakes!"

Our enquiries had by this time exhausted us, and we walked back thoughtfully to our hotel. Next morning we set out to track down the village where a snake-charmer was said to live, and at the end of a long morning succeeded in finding it. Our hopes began to rise.

"There is a snake-charmer who lives in a village nearby," an African informed us. "Her husband is here at this moment. If you take him back to his village in your car, he can arrange for you to meet his wife."

Another surprise awaited us. The snake-charmer's husband was dressed in a well-cut lounge suit. He wore a loud American tie and, more surprisingly, carried a brief-case. He looked more like a city man from New York than the husband of a snake-charmer.

The man fell in with our proposal in a manner which suggested that his wife was photographed every

154

day of the week for television. His attitude put us on our guard at once and Armand asked whether she had traditional clothes.

"Oh yes," the man assured us. "My wife always wears the old-style clothes."

"Good for her," I thought. To my mind it was far more sensible for Africans to wear clothes which had been evolved through the centuries and were suitable for the climate, than those which were highly unsuitable, but European.

With the African on board, we travelled along a rutted road until we came at last to a small clearing in which five or six huts had been built. The clearing nestled between the undulating hills which were bare except for Australian eucalyptus trees planted evenly along the edges of the roads. The Ruanda hills had once been covered with trees, but gradually they had been cut down, and now the hills would be treeless altogether if the Belgians had not started a reafforestation scheme.

"I'll get my wife," said the African confidently, tucking his brief-case under his arm.

A few seconds later, the snake woman came out of a hut, and her husband explained to her what we wanted, but as the explanations continued she shook her head several times. Clearly she was not as keen as her husband to be photographed with snakes. By now we were getting very hungry, and were eager to know whether our mission had succeeded.

Armand said impatiently: "Tell her we only want to photograph her snakes. We don't want to buy them from her. What is her objection to that?"

More palaver followed until, in French, her husband replied: "She says she let her snakes out to graze."

It was a serious moment for us, but the idea of snakes

going out to graze was thought-provoking. Did the snakes wear little bells around their necks like cows? Who watched over them while they grazed, and how were they recalled to the huts? The snake-charmer did not provide the answers. In fact all she would say was that her snakes would not co-operate fully for at least two days. Indeed, she pronounced, the snakes would not allow themselves to be enticed inside her hut unless they had their allotted time in pasture. The situation was highly diverting, but all we could do was to arrange to come back two days later to photograph our performer. She had an expressive face and her gestures spoke eloquently of a mastery of her reptilian pets. Here was the scene we badly needed for our television programme. It would be worth all our trouble: it would be the highlight of our journey to Ruanda.

Before we left, we arranged to pay the lady for her performance, but it came as no surprise to find a disagreement was brewing as to how much she should get. Snake-charmers, we concluded, like many prima donnas, have an inflated idea of their value, but we paid up cheerfully.

I will not dwell on our growing excitement during the next forty-eight hours, except to say that, when we returned, we were convinced that we were about to see the performance of a lifetime.

The lady herself emerged from her hut, looking every inch a snake-charmer. She had magical-looking white marks embossed on her cheek-bones just below the eyes, and four lines painted on her forehead gave her a fierce and frowning aspect. But—to our dismay —only one snake was on view.

Armand at once asked where the others were.

"The others didn't come back from their grazing," answered the snake-charmer's husband.

"Only one!" said Armand, a little crossly. "What is it?"

"A cobra."

The snake-charmer had gathered together a ragged chorus of some sort from the other huts, and some of the girls now began to chant. The charmer grasped a forked stick in one hand, and in the other held a sack, tied at its mouth with rope. Putting the sack upon the ground, she began to dance slowly around it. But it was a lethargic performance. Her gestures lacked the fire we had first seen on the day when she was describing her snakes in order to sell the act.

After a minute or two, Armand stopped filming and said in a resigned voice: "We can't photograph this. It completely lacks spontaneity. Tell her to put some life into it, Michaela."

As tactfully as I could, I passed on Armand's remarks. The snake-charmer listened and immediately went into a completely different routine, but it still bore no relation to what we had seen originally.

"We want life in her movements, not another routine altogether," muttered Armand.

Finally, after watching her for some time we managed to shoot a few feet of the dancing snake-woman, and although not thoroughly happy, we called a halt. The time had now come to ask her to produce the snake. She found another stick and attempted, very clumsily, to undo the knot in the rope with the two sticks. Her efforts were pathetic, and finally, unable to bear it any longer, Armand grabbed the cords from her and undid it himself.

This was the big moment, and we retreated to the cameras to be ready for what the snake-charmer would do next. But she retreated with us, and so did all the chorus girls, a few of them, with little screams, mounting our car. I did not know whether to laugh or cry, but with Armand holding one of her arms, I gently eased our snake-charmer back to where she could be photographed, guiding her by the elbows. The sack had barely moved.

"Take the snake out," I said.

The woman shook her head violently and, trembling, poked the ground with the stick, a few inches from the sack. Nothing happened. She tapped again, and at last the bag heaved convulsively, and then lay still.

At this the snake-charmer would have taken to her heels if I had not held on to her bodily. We struggled for a few seconds before I could calm her down. The panic subsided a little, and Armand took hold of the sack and up-ended it.

The cobra, usually quite a lively snake, dropped on to the ground and languidly, almost insolently, crawled into the bushes. As Armand said—perhaps to graze.

CHAPTER FIFTEEN

ABSENT-MINDED WITCH-DOCTOR

SOME of our most interesting programmes for television have been made in the forests of the Belgian Congo, where there are perhaps more witches than in any other part of Africa.

Witch-doctors, in spite of all that the missionaries have done to put them out of business, are still taken very seriously in Africa. Some use their craft for their own evil purposes, but they are not all villains. I know many who work in exemplary fashion and several whose services are called on by Europeans if anything is stolen or missing. I have in fact called on them myself from time to time, to solve the theft of personal and household goods.

When we visited Sokortugudo, or "Paradise Lake" as it has been christened, I heard a story from Terence Adamson concerning an encounter with a witch-doctor. It occurred while he and a European friend, a medical man, were on safari.

One morning Terence's doctor friend was most annoyed to find that his watch was missing. With Terence's help he searched for it everywhere, but it could not be found and he was forced to the conclusion that it had been stolen. Terence then remembered that a witch-doctor of great repute lived in the very next village on their route. The witch-doctor was summoned. He arrived, imposing in his paint and feathers. With him he had all the paraphernalia of his profession and was ready to go to work at once. He listened to the doctor's complaint, and asked that anyone who could have been in a position to steal the watch should be summoned to his presence.

All the camp followers were sent for and ordered to stand in a circle around him. Squatting in their midst, he eyed them fiercely for some moments and made several incantations. The men watched him with unconcealed uneasiness, shifting nervously from one foot to the other. When he had finished casting his spell he rose to his feet and, taking a handful of powder from a gourd, began to dance slowly around the circle, throwing a pinch of powder into the face of each man as he passed.

On the following day one of the camp followers was seen to be suffering from an eye so badly swollen that the whole eyeball was protruding. Quaking with fear, he came to Terence's friend, confessing that he had stolen the watch, which he now handed back with mumbled pleas for mercy. And there, after an admonitory lecture on the part of the doctor, the matter would have been allowed to rest, had it not been for the fact that the swollen eye stubbornly refused to return to normal.

For two days the doctor tried to cure the swelling, but his efforts met with no success and he was obliged finally to admit that he was completely baffled. Not until then did Terence remember that he had not asked for the spell to be removed. No time was lost in once again sending for the witch-doctor.

Within a short time the witch-doctor was in action again, but on this occasion there was no prolonged ritual. He merely uttered a single incantation and, to the doctor's astonishment, the swelling immediately began to subside. It went down so quickly that the doctor was able to watch the eye returning to normal.

Numa, our serval cat

This forest dweller is an important member of a Congo order. His insignia is a centuries-old necklet of Portuguese beads with a pendant of leopards' teeth

The witch doctresses stamp and posture in their magic dance

Within an hour or two the culprit was completely cured.

From that day the doctor has never fathomed either how the swelling was caused, or how it was cured. As a highly skilled European he had tried every way he knew to treat it, but without effect. Yet, his African counterpart, equipped only with a handful of powder and a few mumbled phrases, had been in complete control of the case.

One of my favourite stories of African witchcraft—a tale which might be called "The Story of the Absent-Minded Witch-Doctor"—was told to me by Noel Kennaway, Northern Frontier District Provisional Commissioner. When he was a junior he had been out on patrol with a detachment of native troops. Rations had run short, and Noel, who hates killing as much as I do, had to decide that a beast must be shot to provide food for his men.

Presently, while the carcase of an antelope was being divided among the troops, an elderly native appeared and asked for a piece of meat. His request was rudely received by one of the soldiers, who pushed him aside and told him to be on his way. The old man mumbled some dark phrases and hobbled off. He had scarcely vanished from sight before the soldier suddenly collapsed in what appeared to be an epileptic fit. He started frothing at the mouth, and his eyeballs rolled upwards until only the whites were visible.

It needed four men to carry him back to camp. All night long he moaned and babbled through tightly clenched teeth, as though he were suffering from lock-jaw. His companions used a twig to try to prise open his teeth in order to force some water down his throat, but the soldier was incapable of swallowing a single drop.

For four days and nights the man lay groaning and helpless. A stretcher was improvised and he was carried on the march, but this practice was such a hindrance to the patrol's progress that Noel decided to establish a small base-camp, where the sick man could be left under guard. Then, with his depleted party, Noel continued on his way.

Some hours later Noel suddenly saw a familiar-looking figure hobbling along the track. It was the old man who had been denied a piece of meat. Noel hailed him as the party drew level. "What did you do to my man?" he demanded.

The old fellow stood deep in thought for a moment, as though searching the recesses of his memory. Slowly he broke into a chuckle.

"Why, imagine that," he said. "I'd forgotten all about him. But maybe it will teach him a lesson after all."

Whereupon he mumbled a few words, bade Noel a polite farewell, and hobbled off down the track. Noel glanced at his wrist-watch and noted the time. He was neither credulous nor sceptical, but merely curious.

When the patrol returned to the base-camp they were greeted jubilantly by the men who had been left in charge of the sick soldier. Seated on a log by the camp fire, with an enamel bowl on his knees and eating ravenously, was the stricken man himself, looking as fit as a fiddle.

Noel enquired when this extraordinarily sudden recovery had taken place, and the time tallied almost exactly with the lifting of the old man's curse.

*   *   *

Witchcraft in Africa finds many manifestations and

162

you are liable to encounter it in the most unlikely places.

When Armand and I were working on location for the film "King Solomon's Mines", we spent a couple of idyllic days at a delightful little inn called the "Pig and Whistle" at Meru. It was set like a jewel high in the mountains, but despite its altitude it was always cosy and warm, with fires in each little cabin and in the dining-room. The inn radiated a feeling of good cheer and well-being, largely due to the charming personalities of the proprietress, Mu Brown, and her son and daughter. Mu took an instant liking to us, and we were made to feel that we were staying with a family of our own rather than in an hotel.

I often thought of the "Pig and Whistle" with warmth and affection, but time passed before I saw Mu Brown again. Our meeting was quite fortuitous— we met in a street in Nairobi—but we greeted each other like old friends.

Over coffee at the New Stanley Hotel, I asked Mu about her family and the "Pig and Whistle", and to my intense surprise she suddenly became grave. The sunshine died in her large eyes and gave place to a mist of sadness.

"We have sold it," she replied slowly.

"But why?" I protested. "It was so much a part of you."

Sadly she shook her head. "We couldn't stay there," she said, trying to control her emotion. "We just couldn't stay."

She clasped her hands tightly and looked away. "You see, we had a murder," she said.

"A murder!" I echoed incredulously—for those were pre-Mau Mau days, and the thought that anyone could have met a violent death at the "Pig and Whistle" was unbelievable.

She nodded slowly. "Do you remember our little *shamba*-boy?" she asked.

The *shamba*- or garden-boy had been a pet of mine, and I remembered him well because of his smiling, good-natured face and his constant readiness to lend a helping hand. He had been young and conscientious as only a country boy in Africa can be. "Surely he wasn't murdered?"

"Oh, no," said Mu, "*he's* in prison now. We are doing everything we can to get him out, but goodness knows if we shall succeed. It's been such a strange and terrible business."

She paused and I waited in silence. It was obvious that she was undergoing a great emotional strain, and I did not wish to prompt her to tell me what had happened if she did not wish to do so.

"It was the Easter week-end. The hotel was packed with guests," she said at length. "In the middle of the night my old houseboy—do you remember him?— came to my room and awakened me, in a state of excitement. 'Come quickly, memsahib,' he said. 'Nyango is dead!'

"The dynamo had been switched off at eleven o'clock, so there was no electric light. I slipped on my dressing-gown by the light of the lantern which the houseboy was carrying, following him downstairs and across the compound to Nyango's hut."

I urged Mu not to continue if it upset her; but she went on as though she had not heard me.

"There were two boys already in the hut when I went in. They were standing just inside the doorway, staring at the bed. Then the houseboy held the lantern higher, and I recoiled at what I saw. For Nyango was

164

lying motionless in a pool of blood, with the head of a six-inch nail—one of a sackful which I had recently bought—jutting from his temple.

"I called the police at once, and they came quickly. They started interrogating all the boys. In every case the answers were the same. Each boy stated with conviction that he had been fast asleep and had heard nothing. It seemed incredible. We could not believe that a man could have been done to death in such a crude and primitive manner without awakening and crying for help. Surely somebody must have heard him? Immediately I suspected Mpishi, our cook, for I knew there was no love lost between him and Nyango. In fact, I had once stopped them from fighting and had seriously considered giving one of them the sack."

Mu paused to sip her coffee which was getting cold.

"When the police had finished their interrogation I suddenly realized that our *shamba*-boy was missing," she said. "I was on the point of informing the police inspector when two African policemen came in, dragging the boy between them.

" 'We found him hiding in the kitchen,' said one of them. 'He was blood-stained.'

"The policemen went on to describe the scene in the kitchen, which was evidently a shambles, and it became obvious immediately that the murder had been committed there and the body dragged to the hut. This at least explained why none of the other boys had heard a struggle. The Inspector turned to the *shamba*-boy and spoke to him sharply. What happened next left us speechless. The boy looked dully at the Inspector, and then, in a lifeless voice, said, 'I killed Nyango.'

"I could not believe it. As far as I knew he had been a good friend of Nyango's—yet here he was, confessing to this ghastly murder. I gazed at him incredulously;

and then, for a moment, I allowed my eyes to travel around the circle of African faces around us. To my astonishment I saw that Mpishi, the cook, was gloating over the *shamba*-boy with a look of vicious triumph. Suddenly he noticed I was watching him, and his expression changed at once. But during that brief moment I felt as though I had actually witnessed the crime and that here was the real murderer."

I could not help asking Mu why the *shamba*-boy should confess to a crime which he had not committed, but all Mu could say was that the boy's eyes were glazed, and he answered the Inspector's questions in a voice which did not seem to be his own.

"Presently the police led the boy away," said Mu. "He went meekly, making no protest, as though he had been robbed of his own free will. His walk was more like that of a zombie than of a human being."

That evening Mu questioned each boy in turn, but although they were less shy with her than with the Inspector, their answers were evasive and she felt convinced that some of them were lying. She ordered them to wash out the kitchen, and decided to close the hotel. The thought of having to superintend meals and being left alone in the kitchen with the cook revolted her.

"I found it impossible to sleep that night," said Mu. "I tossed and turned, and as dawn was breaking, I decided to get up. A few moments later I heard a soft knock on my door. Cautiously I opened it, and in the passage I saw the slim, immature figure of a twelve-year-old boy. I recognized him at once as the young brother of the *shamba*-boy, so I pulled him in and closed the door. He was wide-eyed and nervous, and I coaxed him gently to tell me why he had come. I knew he had something very important to say.

"At length he spoke. 'Mpishi is bad man,' he said, in

a trembling voice. 'He killed Nyango. He will kill again. Mpishi is *mchowi*—he is witch-doctor.' I immediately asked the boy why his brother had admitted to a crime when he was not guilty. His reply was spontaneous and convincing. 'Mpishi put a spell on him,' he said. 'The others are afraid to say what they know because the *mchowi* would kill them too. He was jealous of my brother.'

"Later that morning I reasoned with our old houseboy, begging him to tell me the truth, but he would say nothing. So I tried questioning all the other boys again, and finally I got one of them to corroborate the young boy's story. I went to the police and told them what I had learned. It is up to them now. I can do no more. . . ."

CHAPTER SIXTEEN

HOUSE OF MEMORIES

SOME years ago we had visited the forests of the Ituri in the Congo, the home of those fascinating people, the pigmies. On that occasion we had stayed with our old friend Pat Putnam, who went to the Congo twenty years before, fell in love with the pigmies, and stayed on to look after them. Now, however, we were on a sentimental journey, or perhaps you might call it a pilgrimage, because Pat had died since our last visit, and we wanted to see his old home again.

Pat Putnam, a lovable eccentric, originally came to Africa as an anthropologist attached to an expedition sponsored by an American university. Soon after he decided to stay in Africa he married a girl who was often described as a natural landscapist, and she designed a most beautiful house which was built from the natural materials of the forest and blended perfectly with the grandeur of its surroundings. Not long after the house was finished Mary Putnam returned to New York for a short visit but Pat never saw her again. Within three weeks of leaving him she had died of pneumonia.

After that, he continued to live alone with his beloved pigmies. He was a gaunt, bearded man, and he lived as one of them, eating their food, and hunting with them. He penetrated for miles into the forest and learned the pigmy language. It is a major tragedy that Pat, who knew more about pigmies than any man alive, never wrote a book about them nor passed on his knowledge in any permanent form. When Armand and I first visited him he told us that he fully intended to write a book once he had collected enough material; but he never began to write, and his knowledge died with him.

In later years Pat married again. His wife, Anne Eisner, was an artist who also loved the forest and the pigmies. But a year or so after his death she went back to America and the lovely house was deserted.

We had many misgivings about going back, for the house had been empty for a long time and we fully expected to see the place overgrown and crumbling, engulfed by the relentless march of the forest, reclaiming its own.

But how wrong we were! Within ten minutes of our arrival, a pigmy about the size of a seven-year-old child, who had always been an integral part of Pat's household, ran up to greet us. He had brought his whole family with him.

Proudly he showed us over the house, and we were able to see where the roof had been recently repaired and how clean and tidy the whole place had been kept. The pigmy spoke a few words of Swahili, and I asked him who had been looking after Pat's home so well.

He pointed to himself. "The *bwana* has gone," he said, his eyes large and sad, "but we will always look after the house where he lived."

Armand and I were greatly touched, for Pat's sake. We knew the little man was doing the job without any form of payment out of sheer loyalty to Pat's memory. Pat had been almost a god to them, and when illness struck him down, they often carried him about on a *tepoye* so that he could enjoy the beauty of the forests.

Presently we went to meet our own little pigmies in the forest and were delighted to find that even after the several years which had passed since our last meeting they still remembered us. With great excitement they gathered around, fighting and jostling each other to be the first to greet us. At one moment I had eight of them around me, hugging and cuddling me, showing me new babies which had been born since our last visit and even thrusting the tiny creatures into my arms. The year-old pigmy babies were about the size of an ordinary newly born baby, and they were all as solemn and as dignified as diminutive adults. They clung on to my hands with their tiny fingers and tried to pick the silver nail polish off my finger nails.

We photographed and filmed the pigmies performing a pantomimic dance, and between takes I amused them by showing them some of the dances I had learned in other parts of Africa. It was astonishing how quickly they picked up the steps—they were able to follow any I demonstrated immediately. I taught them Zulu stamping dances of South Africa, which they loved the best; next we tried Indian dances, the rumba, and the Charleston, and at one moment I had a whole crocodile of them behind me doing the conga. I even got them to do some high kicks, but this unfortunately caused great consternation, because one or two of them lost their loin-cloths in the process. Since the pigmies are enormously modest people after their own fashion, the loss of these caused the little people to run screaming into the forest. We returned again to the favourite Zulu dances, and I wondered if they would ever remember all the intricate steps I had taught them. Perhaps some anthropologist of the future will be puzzled to find this particular group of pigmies doing Zulu dances; he may even assume that in the dim and distant past of their history the Zulu tribesmen passed through these dark forests.

For the next shot in which I had to appear I needed make-up, so I took a lipstick out of my bag, and within a matter of seconds I was surrounded by pigmies, all of whom wanted to have red lips. Not only did the girls want to be made up, but also the men, and even the tiniest babies were thrust forward by their mothers. I used more than half a lipstick on them all, but although it was the only one I had brought with me I thought it prudent to cut a further quarter-inch off. Much as I loved the little people I did not dare take the risk of catching any diseases they might have.

Later I unpacked my personal belongings and the pigmies gathered around with great curiosity and excitement. When I produced a pair of high-heeled shoes from a suit-case they gazed at them in wonder. Each shoe was passed round from hand to hand and scrutinized with evident perplexity; my audience apparently could fathom neither the object nor the meaning of the high heels. The only solution was for me to put on the shoes and give a demonstration. When I stood up, three and a half inches the taller, they crowed with delight and enthusiastically clapped their hands. And when presently I slipped them off in order to put on a more serviceable pair, one of the little men came forward and asked if he could try them on.

His tiny feet were completely lost in them, but noticing his disappointed expression I hastened to stuff some cotton-wool into the toes to make a tighter fit. He tried them on again—and what a proud pigmy he became, suddenly towering above his fellows and strutting around like a turkey cock. He begged me to let him keep the shoes, but I felt that to do so might cause jealousy among the others, so I gave him some writing materials and a pencil instead. He was just as pleased, and the shoes were soon forgotten in the wonder of his new possessions. I did a little sketch for him in order to show him how to use the materials. Then I left him seated contentedly on the ground, drawing a series of lines and circles which resembled the style of design which is used on the faces of pigmy women.

Later I went for one last walk with the friendly little people. They led me along one of their small trails with the mighty forest towering overhead. Our voices echoed in just the same way as if we had been walking in some vast cathedral, but surely this forest was far more beautiful than anything that could ever have been designed by man. There was an artless, childlike gaiety of freedom possessed by these little people—a type of freedom which those who are enslaved by a city have never experienced. If only the pigmies are allowed to remain unchanged and unspoiled, they will survive. But will they? I feel immensely sad when occasionally I see one standing at the roadside dressed in white man's clothing instead of his traditional cloth of bark.

Incidentally, it is interesting to find that pigmy women are much sought after by men of the African tribes near whom they live. A good example of the attraction of opposites, I suppose.

There is no indication that the pigmies are softening up as a race, which is something to be thankful for. They have no fear of even the larger animals of the forest and have been known to attack and kill elephants.

Quite recently, as a reprisal for an incident in which one of their number was injured by an Otraco truck, a sizeable band of pigmies mounted an ambush on the road normally used by the Otraco Company, lying in wait for the next truck. I heard this story from the driver. He said a shower of poisoned darts suddenly peppered the sides of his vehicle and one landed inside the cab within inches of his head. He was very lucky indeed to have escaped alive.

During the last walk with the pigmies we passed Pat Putnam's house again for one last glimpse. In my mind's eye I could see his lean, bearded figure standing on the veranda, just as we had last seen him, and I seemed once again to hear those regrettably unfulfilled words of his: "Yes, I'm gathering material for my book."

When passing the house we waved to the pigmy who had so devotedly tended it since his master's death. I only hoped the beautiful place would be allowed to remain as it was, properly maintained and protected from the ever-threatening forest. Perhaps the Government of the Belgian Congo might see fit to preserve Putnam Camp, not only because of its great beauty, but as a memorial to a very remarkable man who was neither a general nor an admiral nor a politician. A man who lived and died among the pigmies and succeeded in penetrating to their very souls.

CHAPTER SEVENTEEN

"THE RAINMAKER"

WE were homeward bound from the Congo after an abortive attempt to photograph some chimpanzees, and Armand and I sat side by side in the truck, the heat mounting through the floor-boards. The soles of our shoes might as well have been made of paper for all the protection they gave us. Armand's face was glistening, and the sweat dripped down his neck into his shirt, leaving ever-broadening patches of dampness on the material. As for myself, I felt as though someone had poured a jug of warm salty water over my shoulders.

Clouds of dust streamed out in the wake of our truck, almost totally obliterating Vincent's vehicle which was following. Vincent, our French driver, had a very prominent nose, pronounced eyebrows and the briefest shorts I have ever seen. Like most of his compatriots he was strongly averse to driving slowly. Consequently, since we did not know this road any too well and had no wish to lose him, we preferred to let him bring up the rear instead of allowing him to career ahead. Looking over my shoulder, I was able to see through the haze of dust that he was keeping a long distance behind, and shortly afterwards I lost sight of him altogether.

"To think," I said to Armand, "that when we set out this morning we were afraid we might get caught in the rain."

We both laughed ruefully, for never before had we seen a countryside more parched, as though it were gasping for water. Even the trees, with dust powdered upon their branches like ashes on the brow of some wizened penitent, seemed as coiled and twisted as though suffering the most agonizing torments of thirst.

Presently we arrived at a small village of mud huts with thatched roofs. It appeared to be deserted, for we drove from one end to the other without seeing a soul. Armand suggested that we should get out and stretch our legs while awaiting the arrival of Vincent, whom we seemed to have left far behind. While we were wandering among the huts we suddenly came across a hunched and wrinkled old crone. She was squatting on the ground with her shrivelled, matchstick legs stretched straight out in front of her. Her dress was a goat-skin, and on her arms she wore a pair of copper bangles. Her head was shaved, but the stubble of her hair which was growing again showed prickly white against the chocolate brown of her scalp.

"Ask her," said Armand, "where the rest of the villagers have gone."

I did not know if she could speak Swahili, but she seemed to understand when I asked her how she was and what was her news.

"I am hungry," she replied, "and the rain has not come."

I translated this fragment of conversation for Armand's benefit, and he asked me once more to enquire where the rest of the villagers had gone.

But the old lady was reluctant to answer my question, so in order to try to win her friendship I sat beside her and talked of other things.

"Have you many children?" I asked.

Yes, she had two sons and a daughter.

"And have they any children?"

"Oh yes, even the children's children have children."

The crone became enthusiastic in the manner that

any grandmother the world over enthuses when you speak of her grandchildren. It is always there—this vital feeling that an old life may be re-lived in the youngest generation—whether in a primitive country or in the artificial environment that we, the Western races, have built around ourselves.

In every woman's heart there is sympathy for those who have passed on the torch of life to others; and so it was, in discussing her grandchildren, that the old native woman and I became firm friends. The discussion went on for a long time and Armand, who could not understand what we were talking about, grew increasingly impatient.

"Ask her," he interrupted, "ask her where the others have gone."

So, when I did ask her for the second time, the old woman pointed westward and said:

"They have gone to the river—to the river which has dried up. They have gone to where the giant fig-tree spreads its arms."

I asked her why, and she looked at me for a long while, as though trying to gauge how much she could trust me. Then, evidently satisfied with what her near-sighted old eyes could see, she said:

"All the people of the village have gone to the giant fig-tree with the witch-doctor to make the rain come."

I translated this to Armand.

"A rain ceremony?" he said, instantly interested. "Perhaps we could photograph it?"

"I'll ask the old lady," I replied, "but I'm afraid they may not like us to see it." I, too, was full of enthusiasm, for the possibility of photographing a genuine rain ceremony was exciting.

"Let's leave the car here and go on foot," said Armand.

Vincent still had not appeared. Although we did not discuss it then, we both felt, as always when dealing with African dogma or religious beliefs, that perhaps Vincent would not be sympathetic towards them and that it would be better if we witnessed the ceremony alone. We knew that when Vincent saw our truck by the roadside he would guess that we had gone off somewhere and would wait for us.

Following the direction the old woman had given, Armand and I set off, but we had gone only a few yards when a small boy, who had obviously been sent after us by the crone to act as a guide, hurried up and beckoned us to follow him. He limped slightly, supporting himself with a long stick, but despite his disability he managed to hop along rapidly. We passed a shrivelled plantation of banana trees, then continued into a dry, tangled mass of bush. As we went we sweated profusely. The pale, opaque sky was the colour of lead, and seemed to press down upon us, giving us a feeling of intense claustrophobia. Through this dry bushland we walked for about a mile, until at last we saw some greener foliage among the grey and lifeless vegetation. In that direction, we guessed, the river, with its life-giving water, must lie; but when we reached it we found it dried up completely. Here and there were holes in the ground where people had dug for water, but in only a few of them was there still an inch or two of moisture.

Commanding the entire scene was a mighty tree which towered above all its neighbours. It was old, gnarled, and twisted, looking almost as though several trees had been gathered together by a giant hand and compressed into a single mass. Beneath this giant were the inhabitants of the village, squatting in a wide circle around seven central figures whose shoulders were moving rhythmically in unison. There were no women, I noticed, in the immediate circle; they were huddled beneath a smaller tree, awaiting their turn in the ceremony.

The little boy who had acted as our guide had left us as we approached the gathering. Hastily I took a scarf from my pocket and pulled it over my head and face. This was a ruse I had used once before, when photographing a circumcision dance in the Belgian Congo which women were not allowed to witness.

"Armand," I whispered, "I shall pretend I cannot see in case we are breaking a taboo. Pretend to lead me."

I could see just as well with the scarf as without, but I purposely made a show of groping and stumbling. As we drew nearer, the sound of the drums and chanting rose with dynamic force. The seven men in the centre of the circle were covered in grey wood-ash, in which wavy lines forming an intricate pattern had been traced. The male natives wore kilts of various animal skins, cut into strips and looking not unlike the apparel of the Zulus. Anklets rattled at their feet as they started dancing round and round in a state of mounting excitement.

As we watched we saw an old, old woman with a calabash in her hand detach herself from the group of women beneath the smaller tree and dance slowly towards the men. She would move forward a few paces, then retreat a little, and then advance slightly further as though irresistibly drawn towards some magnetic field which alternately attracted and repelled her. There was nothing especially remarkable about her costume, which consisted solely of a boldly printed length of cotton falling from her armpits to calf-length.

At last she wove her way into the centre of the circle of dancers, where she laid the calabash on the ground; and then, beckoning to a younger woman who had been hovering outside the circle, she unwrapped the length of imported cloth from her body and handed it to her. We now saw that she was wearing several rows of beads and copper wire around her waist, more threads of beads just below the knees, and an apron-like garment of woven raffia. The naked upper half of her body was decorated with cicatrices in heavy relief—designs which had been carved in living flesh perhaps sixty years previously and which even to this day did not fail to remind one how deep the original cuts must have been.

Taking up the calabash once more, she began simultaneously to dance and to chant. Her shoulders twitched and rolled and shook to the provocative rhythm of the drums; then, in a voice which was remarkably powerful in so old a woman, she asked what was obviously a question in song. Like an echo to the haunting resonance of her voice, there came an answer from the men. And so it continued—question and answer, question and answer—with increasing insistence, while the dancing in the circle became faster and faster.

I watched the old woman closely. She was clearly entranced, for her eyes had rolled back until only the whites were visible and her shoulders shook more and more convulsively. Then the mood changed, and there was suddenly something menacing about the insistence of each question and answer. A cry burbled from the lips of the old sorceress. With the calabash in hand she rocked towards one of the men, tipped a few drops of liquid, which looked like oil, over his shoulders, and then retreated to the centre of the circle. The same

179

action was repeated until all seven men had been sprinkled.

At this the entire character of the ceremony seemed to alter, for those who had been doing the answering now became the inquisitors. The old woman wailed in response, almost as though she were being persuaded against her will. She fell to her knees, then tumbled backwards, and we realized that she was either completely entranced or was having a fit. The chanting was urgent, threatening. Armand and I drew back. It was time, we felt, to make ourselves scarce, so we retreated to the spot where we had left our little guide and returned with him to the village.

"Who was that old woman?" I asked the boy. "A great sorceress?"

"She is the rainmaker," he replied. "She is the rain-doctor of our village."

Armand and I involuntarily raised our eyes to the sky. We could see a few clouds; but the clouds had been there before.

"And what will happen if the rains do not come?" I asked.

"If the rains do not come we will get a new rain-doctor."

"And what would happen to the old one?"

"She would go," said the boy.

"But where?"

He gestured vaguely.

I felt reluctant to question him further, for in my mind's eye I could picture the grovelling and frenzied old woman, and I feared the worst for her if her efforts proved unsuccessful.

It was late afternoon when we returned to our truck and saw that Vincent had caught up with us, for his vehicle was drawn up behind ours.

180

"Shall we stay here for the night instead of moving on?" suggested Armand.

I said I thought it was an excellent idea, for I wanted to be near the old lady. "When the chief comes back we can ask his permission to stay here in the village. Perhaps he'll even lend us a hut."

We waited at the roadside for nearly an hour, but since there was still no sign of any of the villagers returning, and as we did not like to remain in the village without the chief's permission, we drove a few hundred yards up the road and set up our camp-beds for the night.

"Perhaps we should have put up a tent in case the witch-doctor's charms work," said Armand, once we were settled in bed. "We might be flooded out during the night."

But unhappily no such thing occurred. I awoke at first light to the sound of bird-song and saw that the cracked earth remained parched and colourless. There had not even been any dew. Hastily I dressed, and before the others awoke I walked into the village. Could they have killed the old woman during the night? Her charms had not worked, and I felt she was in grave danger.

The village was just beginning to stir. I asked a sleepy-eyed young girl, who was yawning and stretching in front of her hut, if she could direct me to the rain-doctor. But she did not understand Swahili.

The next person I saw was a woman who was sweeping the ground outside her home. "Where is the rain-doctor?" I asked.

She pointed out a certain hut. I hastened towards it and peered inside. The interior was so dark that I almost tripped over a body lying flat upon the ground.

As my eyes slowly became accustomed to the darkness I crouched over the still figure and recognized the rain-doctor. Was she dead? I peered closer, and to my intense relief I saw that her chest was slowly heaving. So at least she was still alive—and that was all I wanted to know. I left the hut at once and hurried back to our camp.

Armand was already up. "Where have you been?" he asked.

"Just to the village," I told him.

"Why so early?"

"I was worried about the old lady."

After breakfast we moved back to the village. Armand and Vincent wanted to see some dances which they had heard about from one of the European administrators, but when they asked the elders of the village if a demonstration were possible they were politely but adamantly answered by a shaking of heads. No rain, no dancing—and that was that.

"Well, we can't go on waiting indefinitely," said Armand.

"Oh, please," I begged, "let's stay at least one day more."

We stayed for three days.

Each morning we gazed at the sky, but still there was no sign of rain.

My fears for the old woman increased, for I knew that magic was a perilous occupation and that in ancient times many an unsuccessful magician had forfeited his life as punishment for failure.

The chief, meanwhile, had lent us two boys to look after our needs. Both of them spoke Swahili, for which I was more than grateful, because through them I was able to hear how the rain-doctor was getting on. I did not voice my fears to Armand and Vincent, but they guessed them. As we sat at dinner that evening, Vincent said:

"I would like to move off tomorrow—as fast as possible."

"Why?" asked Armand.

"Why?" said Vincent. "Because I wouldn't like to be here if there's some kind of incident. These people are strange. They won't wait for ever. In fact, they've probably only waited as long as this because we are here. There hasn't been such a drought for many seasons, and if the rain doesn't come now they'll be looking for a new witch-doctor."

At that moment, as though to underline what Vincent had said, we heard the drums. Usually the drums are beaten on nights when the moon is full, for it is then that the natives dance by its brilliant light. But on this evening there was no moon at all.

A few seconds later, before we had had time to move, a sudden pain shot through my cheekbone into the right side of my nose. I leaped up.

"Rain!" I cried.

They must have thought I had gone mad, but I did not care. I turned to our two boys, who were waiting at the table, and shouted in Swahili:

"Rain! The rain is coming!"

Before anyone could restrain me I ran off in the direction of the drum-beats, closely followed by the two boys.

There was nothing magical about my reaction. Like most supernatural phenomena, it was based on a law of nature. This was something which anyone could understand, provided they knew its causes. Fairly recently my face had been smashed in a motor accident, but an operation by the famous plastic surgeon, Sir Archibald McIndoe, had virtually restored my appearance to normal. Whenever it was damp or threatened to rain, however, tiny red-hot shooting pains wriggle like infinitesimal worms beneath the over-sensitive and newly healed flesh.

When I arrived at the farthest end of the village I saw a circle of three great fires within which a group of men were dancing. The throbbing of drums echoed and re-echoed, reverberating in the night. The animated bodies of the dancers glistened in the leaping firelight, and little clouds of dust spurted up in the wake of their pounding feet. The old rain-doctor had obviously been carried into the centre of the circle on a stretcher, or *tepoye*, which had since been removed, and she now lay there alone, writhing and groaning as she slowly rolled her head from side to side.

I pushed my way towards her through the whirl of dancers; and as I did so I suddenly found myself almost involuntarily joining in the dance. The voices of the singers rose in pitch with excitement and not a little surprise, perhaps, at the sight of this stranger—a barbarian in their midst—entranced by their own magic. My personality dissolved entirely in theirs, as it always does in such circumstances, for there is no such thing as a stranger of a different race or a different background as far as I am concerned when my soul and mind flows and communicates with the stimulus of music. For my part, there was no self-conscious barrier between us. I felt that we were one and the same—my mind, my soul, like a drop of sea-water being poured back into their ocean, all as one. My knees bent and my hands and body shook to the rhythm created by the piercing sweetness of the women's voices, the beating of the drums, and the rich velvet chant of the men's chorus. Slowly, slowly, slowly I bent downwards until my forehead all but touched the old woman's face, then:

"Rain!" I cried.

But there was no response. For a terrible moment I thought she must have lost consciousness or reason on account of her frenzied state. I put out a hand to touch her. I grasped her shoulder and stroked her forehead. And then, mercifully, she opened her eyes and started to mumble a word I did not know. Perhaps, I thought, it meant "rain" in her own language, but I could only guess.

She groaned, and as she slowly rose to her feet, swaying as if to the dance, I looked deep into her eyes. She returned my gaze—and at that very moment I guessed her secret. The wise old sorceress had also had pains in her ageing bones which had told her as plainly as words that rain was on its way. Like all great witch-doctors, great priests, great politicians, she believed in showmanship. She did not rub her back with her hand and say, "My back is hurting—there will be rain tomorrow." Instead, she capitalized on her handicap and made it an asset.

Now, as she danced, she gave an occasional, surreptitious pat where I guessed her pain must have been. We danced in an absolute frenzy, sweating in the heat thrown out by the blazing bonfires. I could see Armand, his face a blur through the dust and smoke, gazing anxiously into the centre of the circle; and I noticed, too, that our two boys had joined wildly in the dance. Time ceased to matter. It was as though one had danced an eternal dance since the beginning of the world.

Suddenly there was a cry and a spluttering hiss, like that of a huge angry cat, as a rain-drop hit the fire.

Then the rain came down.

The dancers, the drummers, old men and women, youths and cripples, the triumphant old rain-doctor and I—we were all clutching hands, laughing, yelling, chattering as the water cascaded down and turned the dust beneath our feet to mud.

Presently, leaving the villagers to their uninhibited jubilation, I took the old lady back to our tent. Armand was already there, lying in bed. He must have been back quite a while, for I did not remember him going. Our two boys made tea and we all crouched down before the dying embers of our fire to drink it in large tin mugs while the rain beat down outside. The old rain-doctor took hers black, laced with four teaspoonsful of condensed milk and several tablespoonsful of sugar. It looked a nauseating mixture, but she drank it greedily. She offered me some snuff, which I accepted against my better judgment and, in consequence, I sneezed loud and long. Finally, I made her a present of two pounds of sugar and some salt which delighted her.

At last she bade me goodnight, to sleep the sleep of the very tired. In her exhausted eyes I seemed to detect the expression of a great tragedienne who has just given the performance of her life. The curtain had just descended, the ovation was still ringing in her ears. And, very humbly, I felt like adding my own applause to the acclaim of the villagers. It had been a thrilling experience and a privilege to witness her triumph.

CHAPTER EIGHTEEN

LAND OF A THOUSAND HILLS

ON a previous visit to South Africa many years before, Armand and I were captivated by the magic spell of Zululand, where we had spent some time. On a journey southward we wanted to try to preserve that magic in films and pictures.

To achieve this we knew we should have to enlist the aid not only of an interpreter but of a man who was both admired and respected by the Zulus, and we were fortunate in finding these qualities combined in one person, a former Native Commissioner named Mr H. P. Braatvedt, who had been born in Zulu country and had written an authoritative book about its inhabitants. He spoke the elegant, involved language, he knew all the customs and etiquette, and he held the Zulus in high esteem, which was fully reciprocated. Both he and his wife radiated charm and kindliness. They were gentle people in the true sense of the word, and we felt privileged to have met them.

We begged Mr Braatvedt to accompany us on our journey into Zululand. Everyone had spoken so highly of him whenever the subject of Zulus was mentioned that we could scarcely contemplate entering the country without him. To our delight he kindly undertook to help us, and it was agreed that he should go ahead to arrange through his many friends among the Zulus for dances, ritual ceremonies, and other aspects of Zulu life to be shown to us.

Thus, for a while, we parted company, but when

word arrived from Mr Braatvedt that all was ready, we drove straight to the little town of Eshowe, which is on the fringe of Zululand.

"It is all arranged," said Mr Braatvedt, his blue eyes sparkling as he greeted us. "A big dance will take place tomorrow morning."

Early next day we drove into Zululand and found ourselves once again in this unique and most captivating of landscapes. As far as the eye could see there were hills. But these were no ordinary hills of varied and irregular shape. They were rounded and moulded in perfect symmetry, like velvety green igloos of giant dimensions, stretching in a profusion of undulations to the far horizon. How rightly has Zululand been called "The Land of a Thousand Hills."

Both Armand and I, as we looked at the landscape, were wondering how the natives would ever find a place flat enough for dancing, but when I put this question to Mr Braatvedt he chuckled. Soon we arrived at the Zulus' dancing place, and the reason for his amusement became immediately apparent.

"The Zulus dance uphill," he explained, "so that the spectators can see them properly."

Brandishing spears and shields, the Zulus looked magnificent in their feathered head-dresses and kilts made of narrow strips of hide. Both men and women were tall and almost plump in a muscular sort of way, with a general air of healthy well-being. The married women wore an elegant coiffure known as the *twala*, which looked almost like a red hat sweeping high and backwards until it widened out into a flat, halo-like crown. The unmarried girls, who did not wear the *twala*, wore costumes which consisted almost entirely of handsome beadwork ropes wound around their hips.

The women sat all around us while the men, having

formed up in line facing us, started performing one of their famous Zulu stamping dances, which are unique. The precision of the steps was incredible. As one man they kicked their legs up high, then stamped first the right foot, retreated a pace or two, and stamped the left. At the same time their bodies postured with superb elegance, their arms moved in rhythm with the stamping of their feet, and their voices rose in a robust and thrilling chant. There was a grandeur and virility about their dances which perfectly befitted their history and the land in which they dwelt.

A Zulu is a man of his word, with a respect for good behaviour which is tantamount to discipline. He cherishes his customs and his language and as a matter of course rebukes his children for expressing themselves in a slipshod way. His code of honour is of a standard which the white races would find hard to emulate. Indeed, when it has come to the breaking of trust and faith in Zululand, it is the European intruder who has usually been guilty. The Zulu himself has never failed to keep his bond, but through broken promises he has already lost two-fifths of his land to the white interloper. One can only hope that new generations will put the old wrongs right, or at least see that the Zulus are protected from any further encroachment.

As the dancing progressed I glanced sideways at Mr Braatvedt. There was a look of pride and affection on his face as he watched the dancers—an expression which mirrored the thoughts of a man who made one regain one's belief in the greatness inherent in humanity. When the performance was over he introduced us to his closest friend among the Zulus—a large man carrying a spherical stomach, with a kindly, open face, a *retroussé* nose, and a radiant smile which was equalled in expansiveness only by those of his twin daughters. This was the first occasion upon which we had ever seen twins among the Africans, for until comparatively recent times it was the common practice to dispose of one of the infants when twins were born. The twins were fine, high-breasted young women of about sixteen, and each wore a short beaded kilt around her slender hips. They were like friendly puppies, and one of them decided to appoint herself our assistant's assistant. Everywhere Des went she carried his equipment for him, and she even became adept at passing him the correct lenses when he indicated them.

Presently we were taken to the hut of our new Zulu friend. It was spotlessly clean and tidy: I could certainly have lived quite happily in it myself. Among the furnishings were some carved wooden head-rests, which also did duty as low seats, and a number of very large cauldron-shaped bowls which were apparently used for holding beer. The interior was spacious, and the acoustics of the domed roof mellowed our voices as we complimented our host on the evident comfort of his home.

Within a short time quite a number of chiefs had assembled outside the dwelling, and they all sat in a circle, with ourselves in the midst, drinking beer from one of the large cauldron-shaped vessels.

The next subject we were hoping to be able to photograph was a ritual involving a witch-doctor, and we were consequently delighted to learn, through the medium of Mr Braatvedt, that two women witch-doctors of considerable and growing fame were to be found nearby. Accordingly, it was arranged that these two women should come to the kraal on the following morning, so that we should be able to meet them.

That evening, when we had left the kraal and driven back to Eshowe for the night, I asked Mr Braatvedt about the status of womenfolk among the Zulus. They had struck me not only as being happy and practically independent, but I had naturally been most intrigued to hear of the existence of women witch-doctors. Was there, perhaps, some measure of equality between Zulu men and women?

"The women have a great deal of independence," he replied, "but they are not allowed to inherit property." And then he started to smile himself. "That is to say, so far as I know, with one exception——"

Mr Braatvedt told us the story of a native woman who posed as a man.

"She came from Natal and was even ostensibly married," he said. "In fact, her wife had several children which had probably been fathered by a neighbour. This woman became a medicine-man and was so successful that she became the owner of much property and cattle. But unfortunately the truth finally leaked out and she was deprived of her property and sent back to Natal."

"What a pity!" I exclaimed. "Does that mean that there can be no such things as a Zulu career-girl?"

"I'm afraid so," affirmed Mr Braatvedt.

"Ah well," I replied, "I suppose a woman is sometimes not so happy being a career-girl. After all, it's quite flattering to have a bride-price paid for you. Armand still owes my mother a few cows."

Armand chuckled. "I wanted to be quite sure that you'd be a good wife," he said. "So I've kept a few head in reserve."

I asked Mr Braatvedt how many head of cattle a Zulu had to pay as the bride-price for a wife.

"An ordinary man pays ten," he replied, "but a

191

headman has to pay fifteen, and there is no limit to what a chief may have to pay."

We arrived early at the kraal next morning, and while we were awaiting the arrival of the witch-doctors our plump and jovial host taught me a number of Zulu dance-steps. We had scarcely begun before his small son, who could not have been more than three feet tall, joined in, and within a matter of minutes a host of small children were all moving in rhythm with us. Armand and Des were so enchanted by the sight of this impromptu dancing-class that they immediately set up the cameras and started filming it.

There was one little girl who was wearing no more than a flimsy girdle of white beads, and as she solemnly went through her paces I happened to notice that her girdle was slipping lower and lower, until suddenly it fell to the ground. The little girl stood quite still, a picture of bashfulness and embarrassment, looking much as a European lady would look if her panties had fallen down in the middle of a very busy street. Our Zulu host immediately stopped his dancing in mid-step and, bending down, carefully pulled up the lady's clothing and adjusted it more securely around her hips. It was done so delicately and with such natural aplomb and dignity that I could not help thinking, once again, what beautifully bred people the Zulus were and what a joy it was to be among them. The little child, whose lip had begun to tremble, did not cry, and the dancing class continued merrily.

We were singing as we danced—"Yesh ye ba, yesh ye ba-ba!"—and while the children and I were being taught how to intone these phrases I saw two strange-looking figures approaching the kraal from a neighbouring hill.

I left the centre of the clearing and walked along a

A particularly fine study of a cow elephant

Buffaloes warning us not to advance

This monitor lizard responded to affection

The prehistoric-looking chameleon

Jock D

little path to greet the two witch-doctors. The first was a strong, buxom woman who might have been any age between thirty-five and forty-five. But the appearance of her elder companion gave me a genuine shock. Apart from her dark skin, she was the living image of my English grandmother. She had the same, rather long, aristocratic upper lip, and the identical, slightly haughty, expression which could be turned on or off as the occasion demanded. As I greeted her she seized my hand and with a deft movement removed my cigarette from the other hand and planted it between her lips.

Both women, of whom my grandmother's dusky double appeared to be the senior partner, were handsomely dressed in fine black cloth embossed with bold patterns embroidered in a darning stitch and edged with coloured woollen tassels. They each wore several necklaces, some of which, I noticed, were the vertebrae of snakes, and when I showed my admiration for them they had no objection to my handling them. The hair of both women was neatly plaited with raffia and hung stiffly to their shoulders, thus producing a sort of beige frame to the brilliant vermilion colouring of their faces.

When we returned to the clearing they wasted no time in getting down to business. The elder woman sat down by herself a little apart from her companion and started mumbling in an undertone. This, Mr Braatvedt explained, was supposed to conjure up the spirits; but Armand, who watched her closely for quite a long time thought she was something of an old fraud. "She mumbles with enthusiasm only when she knows we're watching," he said. It was quite true. She scarcely troubled to open her lips when she imagined that no one was looking at her.

Her companion, meanwhile, began to dance. Tucked

under her arms she carried two wildbeeste tails, mounted and inverted, which protruded like a pair of hirsute, accusing fingers in front of her. As she danced she stamped with an extraordinary exhibition of energy and cried out in a voice which mounted in volume to a vibrant crescendo. The expression on her scarlet-painted face gradually became absolutely rigid, her eyes fixed themselves in a glassy stare, and significant little puffs of dust rose from beneath her furiously stamping feet.

At the height of the excitement the older woman suddenly sprang up and joined in the dance, and it was truly amazing to witness such boundless energy in one so old. She performed exactly the same steps as her younger companion, but if anything did them with more gusto. As they leaped and stamped about the arena they uttered weird phrases in strangely penetrating monotones, and it appeared that whatever was said had some special significance for the onlookers, because their expressions successively registered amusement, surprise, and awe.

All went well with the filming until Armand wanted a close-up of the elder witch-doctor conjuring up her spirits. It could not be done, she said, until she felt moved to do so, and she was adamant in her refusal to co-operate. There followed a few moments of total deadlock until I had the idea of dangling a packet of cigarettes invitingly before her eyes. This did the trick, and for good measure we managed to persuade the two experts to stage the ritual of the "smelling-out" of a criminal or wanted person, though first we were most careful to explain that this was to be a make-believe performance. We certainly did not want to be the unwitting cause of any casualties among the Zulus.

For this ritual a number of men were lined up in

front of the younger witch-doctor, who pranced up and down before them, pointing with the mounted ends of her wildebeeste tails and haranguing the "suspects" until finally, with a cackle of triumph, she picked out the guilty party. It was a highly dramatic performance which left us in no doubt that both these ladies were actresses and show-women of the greatest talent. Although their entire performance had been make-believe it had still been awe-inspiring—even by the most blasé Western standards.

Our film was completed and it was time to say good-bye. We were sorry to leave, for we had made innumerable friends among the Zulus, and they appeared to be just as sad as we were at our departure. Before we left we were presented with a head-rest by the chief, and a pretty little gourd covered with beadwork by one of the girls. When I am back at our home in Kenya I often look at these gifts and think of the delightful and gracious people who live in the south, and at the same time I hope that they may remain unspoiled and unchanged, for their values are such that we may really envy them.

CHAPTER NINETEEN

ADVENTURE ON SEA-LION ISLAND

ON OUR way back from South Africa, Armand decided we would try to photograph sea-lions for one of our television programmes.

We have always been fascinated by sea-lions. In fact, Armand regards them as being among the most intelligent of animals, and it is a terrible thought that human beings can have so little mercy as to kill them in a brutal and savage manner. I would never wear the fur of a sea-lion any more than I would dream of helping hunters in their ghastly work by disclosing the location of a paradise where these beautiful creatures live and play to their hearts' content.

We had embarked in a small motor-launch with the intention of photographing sea-birds on various large outcrops of rocks, which jutted like mailed fists from the offshore waters. Eric, the owner of the launch, was a man who loved animals, and being an expert navigator, he was able to give us a grandstand view of all the natural life that was to be seen. We circled round for a time, photographing many varieties of sea-birds. But the water was choppy and Armand feared his pictures would be spoilt by the rocking motion of the boat.

Then Eric suggested something which pleased us enormously. Would we like to see a really extraordinary sight? Of course we would!

"But first," he went on seriously, "I must ask you to promise never to tell a single soul where it is."

We promised.

Accordingly, he swung over the tiller and we headed out to sea. The water soon became still more choppy, and although Armand and I are good sailors we began to feel a little uncomfortable. Presently, however, our interest in physical discomfort was distracted by the sight of a rocky island, much larger than any we had yet seen, jutting out of the water straight ahead of us.

We circled around it—a rather difficult manoeuvre because the rock surface was in places covered by only a few inches of water. But Eric is a skilled seaman, and he steered his small craft through this tricky passage with all the confidence of an errand boy riding his bicycle without using his hands. Within a few moments we found ourselves entering a small natural bay, almost a lagoon, which had been quite invisible from the sea on account of a smaller island blocking it from view.

I shall never forget the sight that met our eyes!

Hundreds of sea-lions were disporting themselves on ledges of rock worn smooth through the basking, frolicking, and mating of countless generations of their forbears. Large bulls were surrounded by their harems, while small pups with wide, blue, almost myopic-looking eyes frisked and flopped in the shallows.

A young bull, we saw, had enticed a female to the very edge of her husband's territory, and it looked as though the couple would make good their escape when suddenly the husband glanced round and spotted them. It was astonishing to see how quickly he moved. As his massive bulk thundered across the slabs of rock he uttered an indignant bellow—a cross between a bark and a roar—which stopped the fugitives in their tracks. For a moment it seemed that the young bull might attempt to defy the threat of his senior; but alas, his lady remained stock still, as though petrified by fear, and showed no further inclination to flee with him.

The two males were left face to face, swaying in front of one another with whiskers bristling, until suddenly the old bull charged forward and his young rival slithered with undignified haste into the water. The young wife, looking abjectly penitent, then received a reproachful slap from her husband, who gave her a slight nip on the neck and herded her back into the centre of his family circle.

"We've simply got to photograph this," exclaimed Armand, with delight. "But it can't be done from the boat. Can we land?"

"I've only been ashore once," Eric replied, "and they all flopped into the water as soon as I landed. They didn't come back for hours . . ."

"Let's circle round the smaller island," Armand suggested.

I could guess what was in his mind. I tried to conceal my anxiety, for much as I disliked the idea of attempting the perilous landing on the jagged rocks, it was still more disturbing to think of Armand doing the job alone. I have always felt that we should face danger together. Armand read my thoughts—and he knew of my fear of water.

"You know you don't need to come with me, darling," he said.

But I begged him to let me come. I told him I could pass the lenses and help a little.

"I'm not sure anyone could land on that rock," said Eric. "Anyhow, we couldn't do it without a dinghy. I'll bring mine out on tow tomorrow. But I warn you, it's going to be extremely tricky."

As he spoke we could see the waves hurling themselves like massive fists against the rock, as though intent upon hammering it into the sea.

"You might stand a better chance of landing on the side facing inland," continued Eric. "It's slightly less rough over there. But we ought to have another pair of hands with us to row the dinghy and help unload—and there's only one man I'd trust with that job."

He was referring to his brother, Gee, who was possibly the only other person who knew of the existence of the lagoon. Gee, we learned, was due to arrive from the city on the following morning. "He's got some business on hand during the day," said Eric, "but we could land you on the island in the morning and call back to pick you up in the afternoon."

This suggestion suited us admirably.

We were up in the morning early with everything ready for the trip—camera equipment, a tin of water biscuits, a jar of butter, and a thermos-flask of hot coffee. Eric and his brother met us, and Gee turned out to be a short, stocky man who was much the older of the two. He appeared to be quite annoyed when he learned that we were going to visit the island, but Armand quickly assured him that we were both just as keen to protect animals as he and Eric.

"I'm glad to hear it," he said, with obvious gratification.

We set off. The sea, as Armand observed, was slightly less choppy than on the previous day, but Eric was unimpressed.

"It may look fine now," he replied, "but you can never trust the sea."

It was only when Armand, Gee, and I were already in the little dinghy that I realized how tricky it was going to be to land on the rocks. The sea-lions were gazing at us inquisitively, and some of them were even circling around us. It seemed almost as though they were carrying on a conversation among themselves in their hoarse voices: "Who are these strange animals? What are they going to do?"

Armand went ashore first, and we threw him the nylon rope we had brought with us. He tied his end to a rock while Gee secured the other to a seat in the dinghy. It was now my turn to go and I felt sick with fright, for I saw that Armand was wet almost to the waist and I had a horror of plunging out of my depth. However, it was no use worrying, so under Gee's guidance I managed to get out of the dinghy and lower myself into the water. Clinging to the rope with one hand and to the side of the boat with the other, I felt hopefully with my feet for a solid foundation. But when finally I did touch rock bottom the water was up to my armpits, and with every motion of the sea it mounted as high as my hair. Clinging frantically to the rope, I surged forward.

"Bravo!" called Armand. "You've almost made it! A few more steps—and don't let go of the rope!"

"That I'd never do," I muttered to myself.

And at the very next step I vanished below the surface. One moment my feet were on solid rock, and the next there was nothing to support them. It was the sort of sensation you experience in a dream when you miss a step and feel you are falling through space. The water rushed over my head, but grimly I clung to the rope and struggled forward, hand over hand, trying to hold my breath though my lungs were bursting. Then suddenly, mercifully, a hand clutched me. It was Armand. He hauled me spluttering on to the rocks.

Fortunately, in the water-tight floating boxes which had been constructed for our camera and equipment, we had also packed our food and a change of clothing.

"We'll be back in the afternoon," called Gee, as he pushed off and started rowing back to the launch.

Armand and I waved goodbye, then quickly changed into dry clothes and set to work. Most of the sea-lions had remained on the other island, but there were nevertheless several which had come closer to observe our landing.

"This is wonderful material," exclaimed Armand. "Absolutely unique—I have never seen sea-lions so tame."

It was true, and we soon became so preoccupied with our work that we scarcely noticed the time go by. At noon we broke off for a brief snack and cups of hot coffee, and then resumed our work. The sea, meanwhile, had become more choppy, and a cool breeze had sprung up. Feeling a little chilly, I pulled my cardigan out of one of the containers and slipped it on. Armand, too, was beginning to feel the cold, so I handed him his sweater.

"They are late," he muttered, pulling it over his head. "I should have expected them back by now."

"Armand!" I cried. "Look!"

But he had already seen it. Our biscuit-tin had been swamped by a wave and was being carried out to sea. Scrambling down the rock, Armand tried to grab it.

"Don't bother—there are only a couple of biscuits in it," I called, afraid that he might be swept off the rock by the wash. But he had already managed to retrieve it as it was carried in by the next wave.

As he turned to face me his eyes were grave. The position was serious.

"I left the tin high on the rock," I said. "The tide must have turned."

We looked all around us. We had been so engrossed

in our work that we had not noticed that our vantage point had grown perceptibly smaller. Hurriedly we carried our camera and equipment to the highest point on the rock. It was a steep and difficult climb, and we constantly slipped and stumbled as we struggled up the jagged surface.

"This is bad," said Armand.

Our clothes were being ripped to shreds and our hands were cut and bleeding.

"Something must have happened to them," I said.

We sat huddled on the summit of the rock. Armand curled his arm around my shoulder. The waves had increased in ferocity, and a biting wind whipped the cold spray into our faces.

"Let's pack the equipment," suggested Armand.

At least it gave us something to do.

It was already dusk, and dark clouds were mounting in the eastern sky. A nocturnal bitterness seemed to ride towards us on the waves, fumbling at the rock with icy fingers.

"We may as well finish up the food," I said. "It'll be one thing less to carry."

Although neither of us said it, we both knew that unless help arrived soon there would be little chance of our surviving until morning. We sat in silence and ate what could have been our last meal; and as we did so a massive wave, like a hungry tongue, swept over what was left of our rock and almost reached our feet. I think we both realized at that moment that the rock would be totally submerged during the night, if not sooner.

I turned to Armand. "Darling," I murmured, "you had better swim to the other rock. You might be able to make it—and perhaps they will come before this one is completely covered."

He looked away, and I saw a muscle throb in his neck. It was not until he had regained mastery over his voice that he turned to me and said:

"You know I would never leave you here alone, so why talk about it?"

I begged him to go. "You know I couldn't swim so far in a sea like this," I said.

"No swimmer could."

I did not quite believe him, but at the same time I knew that I would not have deserted him if our roles had been reversed. I stood up to stretch my cramped limbs, and as I did so a giant wave surged up and swept me off my feet. I felt myself being carried away, sucked under by the foaming, seething wash, and clutched frantically for anything that might arrest my slithering fall. Then suddenly I felt a strong grip on my arm, and Armand dragged me back to safety, however temporary, on what was left of the rock.

It was bitterly cold, and our soaking clothes clung coldly and clammily to our shivering bodies. Our teeth chattered, and our limbs grew numb. With longing I dreamed of a bowl of hot soup, but hastily put the thought from my mind. Our personal discomfort had become so acute that we could not even think of the danger we were in. The wind howled, and the icy spray showered all over us. Every now and then, when a wave washed over our feet, we shifted our position to another part of the rock. But what, I asked myself, was the use? It was only a matter of time, it seemed, before we were both overwhelmed by the waves and sucked under the surface.

It was quite dark now, but mercifully a pale moon shone through the gathering clouds. At first we talked of small things and reminisced about the many happy and exciting years we had spent together. But presently we relapsed into silence, preoccupied with our private thoughts. I glanced at Armand, wondering if he could possibly have fallen asleep. And at that moment I suddenly heard it—or thought I heard it. My heart raced wildly.

"Armand, can you hear it?"

He was gazing seawards.

"Hear what?"

And as he spoke he heard it too—the muffled throb of motors.

"The launch!"

At risk of tumbling into the water I stood up and wildly waved my arms, and we both started shouting at the tops of our voices:

"Here! We're over here!"

As we strained our eyes we were gradually able to discern the hazy silhouette of the launch as it loomed out of the moon-bathed darkness.

"Over here!"

We could see a shadowy figure clambering into the dinghy and then a voice came riding over the waves:

"It's all right! We're coming!"

This time it was Eric who brought in the dinghy.

"Thank God we weren't too late," he called, as soon as he spotted us perched upon the rock. "We had a breakdown. Couldn't get the darned engine going again."

He rowed in as closely as he safely could and threw us a rope. I wanted to get the camera and equipment, including the precious films we had taken, aboard the dinghy first, but Armand would not hear of it.

"To hell with that!" he exclaimed, turning upon me. "You'll go first!"

But I had my way, and it was not until our photographic material was safely aboard that Armand and I, with teeth chattering and our bones frozen to the marrow, made our escape from the pinnacle of rock which had been our prison and had almost been our gravestone.

CHAPTER TWENTY

OF LIFE AND DEATH

THE rains had ended at last, and Armand and I were exploring the plains in our open jeep. We drove slowly, for even with four-wheel drive, the jeep was difficult to manoeuvre over the still soggy ground. Each change of season brought fresh surprises and excitements, and we were very much aware that these secrets would not be revealed to us alone, but through our cameras we could share them with millions of other people.

The landscape was typically East African: savannah interspersed with islands of thornbush and brush and occasional clusters of flat-topped trees. Everything looked new and fresh, the green of the grass was meadow-like, and all the bushes and trees had broken into new life. The sounds were those of young life assured of a plentiful food supply, and we expected to see cubs, foals, young baboons, and fledglings of all kinds.

Armand slowed down and came to a stop. For some time he had been looking from side to side, and I knew something had attracted his attention.

"Pass me the glasses, Michaela," he said. I took them out of their case and handed them to him, but although I looked in the same direction, at first I saw nothing unusual. There was a low patch of brush and thorn a few hundred yards away, a very slight gap, and then more thorn. My eyes travelled further to the left. There again was another patch of thorn, curiously like a wall. It looked natural, until one compared it with the other islands of bush on the savannah. Something struck a wrong note; was it too long, too regular in shape? And yet it was broken here and there with clumps of thorn trees. We might have passed it a dozen times and not noticed anything odd, but where we had stopped a trick of the light showed up the artificial arrangement of the massed thorn and brush.

Armand passed me the glasses without comment. I looked and saw the horns of an antelope barely showing above the grass. A sitting antelope; that again was odd, for an antelope would surely never sit in a place which gave such good cover for lions and other predators. When they rest, they like to be able to see all around them. I lowered the glasses and glanced questioningly at Armand.

"That barricade is man-made," he said. "I don't like the look of this. Let's go and investigate."

We altered course and drove towards the barrier. The nearer we went, the more natural it looked. Had we been deceived by a trick of the light? We left the jeep and examined one of the bushes closely. The base had been cut and cunningly intermixed with other branches to make a dense mass. Armand looked grim. He led the way back to the jeep and we drove slowly along parallel with the barrier.

As we neared the antelope I wondered why it did not jump up and bound away at the sound of our engine. My heart contracted, and I felt a surge of sickening disgust and fear. The smell of death and decay came forcefully towards us, surrounding and permeating our very bodies. The smell of death always makes me cringe, and now I had to fight a desire to vomit as we looked at the horrible sight before us. The effort brought tears to my eyes as I looked down.

The antelope was a Grant's gazelle—or had been a

Grant's gazelle. The eyes had been pecked out by vultures; the neck was bloated and bulged above the bloody cord that bound it. A wire cord. Out of a fearful wound, torn because of the creature's desperate efforts to escape, writhed maggots an inch long. Bold and powerful now on the pitiful remains of their victim, how long ago had they started their macabre feast? Certainly when it was still alive, and fighting death. The death must have been quite recent, but, because of the tropical sun, decomposition had set in rapidly. The animal's tongue protruded from the poor parched lips, crawling now with flies. We saw where the noose had been cunningly placed in a gap in the camouflaged fence, and the antelope, unsuspecting, had been caught when bounding through it.

"There's nothing we can do," said Armand, answering my unspoken question. "At least, nothing we can do for *this* poor beast."

We got back into the jeep silently, and drove slowly along by the side of the barrier again. We were only two hundred yards away when we saw a partly eaten zebra carcass. The underside of the belly was still uneaten, which indicated that lions had not been feeding from it, but one back flank up to the knee had been eaten away and the splintered bones showed that a hyena had found a meal. Although the animal had turned and twisted in agony, the imprisoning noose had not broken; again, the neck showed terrible wounds, but not deep enough to kill mercifully.

I knew of poachers and so did Armand. We had been told of the horrors which attended the death of the animals, but the sight and smell of such a death, seen at first hand, had a more terrible impact than hearsay.

"But if they are hungry enough to kill these animals," I asked Armand in bewilderment, "why don't they come back for the meat?"

"They don't kill for meat. Only for tourist trophies," he said. He beckoned me closer, and it was then I saw that the corpse had been mutilated; the tail had been hacked off at the base of the spine. At once I thought of the piles of zebra tail and wildebeeste tail fly-whisks in Nairobi's market, of the trays of whisks in the tourist shops of Delamare Avenue and Government Road, and shuddered. They were priced at a few shillings each, and made amusing presents to take home to Boston, Vienna, London, or Manchester. Surely, if the kind, ordinary people who fingered this merchandise could have felt the agony of the poor beast through their fingertips, they would have wept for shame? That was the terrible part of it: these people, kind and gentle probably, were the very people who made this filthy trade lucrative. They were the unwitting cause of this wholesale brutality.

We passed more pitiful corpses of several kinds of animal, until at last we came to a tiny Thompson's gazelle, the friendly little Tommy with its restless tail and dainty hooves. The foreleg of her dead fawn lay at her feet, while part of the intestines had been dragged into the grass, half-eaten by a baboon or some other scavenger. The fawn had been too young to leave its mother—she, caught in the dreadful snare, had tried desperately to save her young, the trampled grass and the thorns stuck in her coat told us as much. She was still standing on her feet, emaciated, her neck stretched agonizingly in the noose, which held her head within a few inches of the ground.

"Armand, she's still alive," I managed to say.

Quickly we jumped out of the jeep. "If only we had

a gun," said Armand. "At least we could put her out of her misery."

But we never carried guns, and in all our years of travelling this was the first time I wished we had. For although neither of us were killers, either of us would have put that little victim out of its misery.

Armand supported the gazelle, while I ran back to the jeep and searched in the tool box for wire cutters. We managed to cut the wire and carried the tiny animal back to the jeep; she weighed no more than a baby. Armand probed gently into the bloody pulp of her throat, feeling for the deeply embedded wire. The weary little head sank on my knee and blood from the gangrenous flesh oozed on to my trousers. I was crying by this time, and Armand himself was not far from tears. We moistened her lips with water and started back to camp: I sat in the back of the jeep, holding her head in my lap. She died before we arrived, but I like to think that at least she died more peacefully than she would have done if we had abandoned her. We had done all we could . . . for the moment.

"Yes, I know all about it. You can't tell me!" We were sitting in a friend's office. Dick was one of the few —far too few—game wardens who look after the African wild life, and we had gone to him as soon as we could break camp.

Dick sat back in his chair and surveyed us, half in exasperation, half in sympathy. "I get these stories all the time from people, but what can I do about it? In my area of nearly two million acres, all I have is seven men with two bicycles between them to chase off poachers. It's during the rains, of course, when we can't get in on patrol, that the beggars are most active. They even set up camps here in my park and use them as bases. Would you believe it, there've been bands of as many as seventy men setting snares and building the sort of brush barricades you came across. They're skilful blighters, cunning, too. What can seven men do against such odds?"

"There must be something," I said helplessly.

"Look," said Dick. "Here are some facts. In two years two thousand elephants were destroyed in Tsavo Park alone—a National Park, mind you—by poisoned arrows. We manage to arrest one of the poison peddlers occasionally, and we've found that one poison container costing ten bob is enough to kill a hundred animals. Work that out in pence and you'll see how cheap life—and death—can be!" He tapped his pencil on the desk and drew a deep breath. "Did you know that one hundred and eighty thousand head of game *a year* are killed by poachers in the one National Park Tanganyika has? And this problem doesn't only crop up in British territory—the game is being literally wiped out in the Congo, in Uganda, in French Equatorial Africa, wherever there is any game left."

The three of us sat silent. What could we do about it by ourselves?

But we three were not alone after all. All over Africa were people who thought as we did. The proof came some time later, when we met a dark-haired, clean-cut young man, whose name was Noel Simon.

After the introductions he began to speak eagerly. "I've been wanting to meet you both for a long time," he said. "I bought a farm in Molo when I left the R.A.F. I had always wanted to live in Africa, ever since I was a boy—you know, all those wild animals. . . . I'll never forget the thrill it gave me to see the first bush buck on my own land. I used to keep a checklist of all the animals I saw every day. I expect that sounds very foolish. . . ."

"Of course not," I said warmly. "There's nothing so wonderful as watching wild animals in their natural surroundings."

He flashed me a smile.

"Well, soon I noticed there were fewer year by year. There had been so many animals roaming about—and of so many kinds—when I first came. I couldn't understand what was happening. I had 'No Shooting' notices all over my property, of course, but the animals still disappeared. It worried me so much in the end that I found the farm was taking second place in my thoughts. I had to do something about it. . . . So I left Molo and came to Nairobi to talk to people from the Game Department, the National Parks, Locust Control—anyone at all who I felt had the opportunity of observing game. Yes, they'd all noticed it, the game was disappearing. They each gave different reasons. Some thought that industrialization was encroaching on the animals' natural haunts, others that legal hunting was to blame. But when I checked with the Game Department, the number of licences issued didn't seem to account for such a decimation."

"What about biltong hunters?" Armand put in.

"Well, yes. They, too, are certainly responsible for a part of the alarming decrease of wild life. . . . But soon it was apparent that poaching, by whites and blacks—difficult to control because of lack of adequate police personnel and financial resources, and dealt with far too leniently by the courts—was the main agency of destruction. Soon it became clear to us that if what remains of the wild life of Africa was to be saved, it would be necessary to arouse public opinion, to make known the danger, to stimulate action. . . ."

"I feel you're doing something positive about it, then," I said.

Noel nodded. "That's what I wanted to see you about," he said. "We are forming a Wild Life Society here in Kenya. There are about twelve of us at present —the Blochs, Donald Kerr and Sid Downey, Abdul Ghafur Sheikh . . ." he mentioned a few more names. "They're in it with me. Can I count you in too?"

"Whole-heartedly," we said together.

Since then the Wild Life Society of Kenya has grown from its few founder members, and now numbers several thousand members all over the world. It is still growing fast; it is playing an increasingly important and effective part towards conservation, and the protection of wild life; the larger it grows, the more hope there is of preserving the last remnants of the fabulous fauna, once so exuberantly rich, of Africa.

At least, I felt, I had not cradled that dying gazelle's head on my knee in vain.

CHAPTER TWENTY-ONE

A DELAYED DEPARTURE

ONCE again we were leaving Africa, this time bound for Asia and the East, a journey that would take us many thousands of miles away from our plains and forests and introduce us to many unfamiliar and fascinating sights and sounds. But the longest journey starts with the first step, and our first step meant the drive to the airport at Entebbe, to catch a plane to Nairobi. There we would change planes for Aden.

We were late. Last-minute packing and last-minute purchases at the local *duka* had delayed us as usual; Armand was in first gear and impatiently ready to let in the clutch while I was trying to fit myself among the suitcases and packages in the jeep. A car drove up and stopped with a squealing of brakes; a large florid female form, shouting "Stop! Stop!" and making agitated signals struggled out of it and ran towards us. I saw Armand hesitate, but he took his foot off the throttle, controlling his feelings by a visible effort.

A hand reached in and grasped my arm. It belonged to the stout, panting lady who, now she had attracted our attention, stood and gasped for breath. At last she said, as we gazed at her in amazement, "Please, oh please, will you help me? I'm Mrs Fosdyke."

The voice that came from that large body was pitifully small, and Armand was impelled to ask what she wanted.

"Oh, my dears," she said, holding her side. She was obviously unused to her recent exertion. "My dears,

214

you are the only people I could ask this favour from. It's a miracle, an absolute miracle to have caught you. . . . You're going to Entebbe, aren't you? Then will you take my little darlings? I've no one to look after them, you see—I'm going on leave, and . . ."

"My dear madam, we are flying to Arabia," said Armand, starting to engage the gears.

At this Mrs Fosdyke dug her fingers deeper and more painfully into my arm. She looked ready to burst, either with breathlessness or emotion, or both.

"You can't," she cried. "Oh, you can't refuse! All I'm asking is for you to take them to Entebbe and you'll be met by my friends the Glossops. They're going to look after them for six months, while I'm on home leave."

By this time I was full of curiosity to know who or what her little darlings were. Elephants or mice, children even?

Armand said crisply, "I'm sorry, Mrs Fosdyke. There just isn't room for anything in this jeep. We're packed tight as it is." He spoke the truth. We were jammed to the roof with luggage and equipment. Again he tried to start the jeep, but as it moved slowly forward, Mrs Fosdyke gave a squeal of despair and jumped right off the ground, hanging over the side on top of me. Were we to drive to Entebbe like this? Armand stopped the car, and began to look angry.

She started to speak again, her feet once more on the ground. I watched her, fascinated, and moved my numbed arm. She must be very attached to the little darlings, whatever they were, to take so much trouble, and risk such unpopularity for their sakes.

"But they're so small!" she was saying. "So small! They're tiny, the darlings, and they've never bitten anybody, never!" She darted away to a car parked

215

nearby. An African got out of the back of it, carrying a large wooden box. Mrs Fosdyke ran back to us, repeating in an agitated voice, as she caught Armand's sceptical glance at the size of the box, "They're really tiny, the box is much bigger than they are."

"What are they?" I asked at last.

"Two tiny little monkeys," she said triumphantly. "I fed Oggie with a fountain-pen filler when he was a wee baby and no one thought he would live."

This I couldn't resist. "Armand," I said, "we only have to take them to Entebbe. This lady's friends will meet us there."

Armand gave a strained smile. "All right," he said. "We'll take them if we can make room somehow." He looked sternly at Mrs Fosdyke, now bobbing in the roadway with pleasure and gratitude. "Remember, madam, our responsibility ends when we reach Entebbe. We simply must catch that plane."

"Oh, God bless you, I knew you would!"

I was enveloped in a warm hug. When I was freed, I turned to look at our travelling companions, which had now reached us. I smothered a gasp. Maybe the little darlings had once been small enough to be fed with a fountain-pen filler, but that time was long past. Two sturdy half-grown vervet monkeys in their box returned Armand's sardonic stare. Already they had all the worldly sophistication of adult monkeys.

The larger one, after this first visual encounter, crouched down, lowering his lids over his fierce yellow eyes. He twitched nervously, then his eyes widened and he sprang at the chicken wire at the front of the cage and shook it, baring his teeth and making hostile monkey noises. This at once sent the smaller one into a fury. She attacked her companion in a kind of nervous hysteria, which stopped as suddenly as it had begun,

216

and turning her back abruptly, she searched irritably through the fur on her forearm.

Mrs Fosdyke's mouth dropped open in dismay. "I expect they're upset," she said. "They know, the poor little dears, that their mother is going to leave them for six months."

I dared not look at Armand. Trouble was ahead, I felt it as acutely as his unspoken reproaches which bristled around me. But we could not go back on a promise. The box was stowed aboard. In order to get it in, my camera case was transferred to the space on the floor between my legs and the seat. Experience told me that this would be painfully unsatisfactory, but there was no other arrangement possible and I longed to be off. After all, I had got us into this predicament and now had no right to complain.

We waved goodbye to Mrs Fosdyke, who stood gazing after us with a triumphant smile on her plump face. She was waving a handkerchief, but whether to us or the monkeys I couldn't make out. For some time we drove along in silence, then I ventured to glance at Armand; he returned my look sternly at first, then suddenly his mouth twitched into a smile and we laughed for three minutes without stopping.

"What *will* you do next, Michaela?" he said at last.

I was indignant. "It's all your fault," I countered at once. "You shouldn't have let her talk me into it."

"I was waiting for that!" Armand exclaimed. "Well, never mind, we've got them now. I only hope those friends of hers will be at Entebbe; we'll have no time to spare when we get to the airport."

An hour later, as we were passing a group of young African girls carrying bananas on their heads, a shrill clamour broke out at the back of the jeep. Armand stopped at once. We both knew what that meant. When two monkeys made that kind of noise one of them was going to get seriously hurt before long; their sharp teeth could bite off a finger or badly maul a leg. We had taken many an injured monkey to the vet to be stitched up after a battle. The travelling box rocked with the fury of the antagonists and the girls paused in their single-file march to watch us as we both dashed round to the back of the jeep. They gathered round in an awed circle as we tried to separate the monkeys.

"It's no good, they'll kill one another," said Armand. "Do you mind having one of them on your lap?"

I didn't like the look of the well-displayed fangs of Mrs Fosdyke's little darlings, but there was nothing else we could do.

"All right, Armand," I said; "let me fetch a dog-lead from the glove box." We always carry dog-leads, for we never know when we might have some enticing pet offered to us for sale by Africans we meet along the roads. Armand cautiously opened the door of the box and grabbed the nearest monkey, holding it firmly with its arms behind its back, so that it could not bite. The little creature looked like a rowdy drunk in miniature, its bad-tempered little face screwed up in hatred.

We managed to attach the lead to a belt it luckily wore around its waist and settled into our seats once more. As we drove along the little monkey's temper evaporated so far as I was concerned, and it snuggled in my lap like a child worn out by its own naughtiness. But it still bore a grudge against Armand. When my handbag slid off the seat on to the floor and Armand reached down with one hand to put it back on my lap, it was up in a flash and sank its teeth into the back of his hand.

Armand bound up the wound, which bled considerably, with the last of his clean handkerchiefs, carefully kept to be on show in the plane to Aden.

Our journey after that was fairly peaceful, apart from the minor discomfort of having my knees wetted twice. There was a short, sharp shower just about midday, and the little monkey huddled close to me under my plastic raincoat. She found a new game, from which she refused to be distracted. This was tearing small holes in the material, through which she peeped up at me.

Towards late afternoon we stopped half a mile from the hotel, and decided to put our little terror back with her companion in the box. We hoped that they would forget their enmity at night time, and huddle together for warmth, for monkeys are clannish creatures. Another reason was that many hotels have a prejudice against monkeys, and we hoped to smuggle them up to our room as unobtrusively as possible.

We untied the box and put it on the ground. Armand opened the door cautiously with his uninjured hand and told me to put the monkey inside. But by this time she had become thoroughly attached to me, and refused to let go. I struggled to pinion her arms behind her back and Armand was helping to put her in when with an agile twist of her body she turned in the doorway and bit his other hand. The pain and shock made him let go of the door, and in a second both monkeys had whisked out and were away.

"Follow them," shouted Armand, nursing his hand. But they were off in different directions. "Go after the small one, Michaela," he called, starting off after the larger male. I ran after the little one I had been nursing, but after a few yards she shot up a tree and clung to a branch well out of my reach, grinning down at me. Our short-lived friendship was forgotten, and she chattered indignantly. Armand was no luckier.

His monkey had also climbed a tree and now sat high up, jeering down at him.

We were within shouting distance of each other, and there we stood, the darkness falling, half a mile from the comfortable beds in the hotel, staring up into our respective trees. We dared not leave our charges, for if one of them managed to climb down and run away, the other would follow. There was also the possibility of wild monkeys luring them away, and still more the possibility of prowling leopards, notoriously fond of monkey meat. I thought of Mrs Fosdyke, and in desperation tried to climb the tree to reach her errant darling. All this provoked was a bad-tempered outburst of chattering.

Large drops of rain started to fall, and I remembered my tattered plastic raincoat. The jeep wasn't far; perhaps I could creep quietly away and fetch it? The monkey had been quiet for some minutes, and might even be asleep. But after I had gone a few cautious steps she gave a sharp, warning alarm cry. I gave up and sank down on the wet ground under the tree. It was now quite dark, so I called across to Armand to ask how he was getting on.

"Settling in for the night," he called back. "Are you all right?"

"Fine," I answered through gritted teeth. "I only wish Mrs Fosdyke was here!"

Armand's only reply was a bitter laugh.

I was very hungry by this time and automatically felt in my trouser pockets for cigarettes and matches. To smoke would at least take the edge off my hunger. Then, guiltily, I remembered I had given up smoking three weeks ago, so there was not even this consolation.

The darkness settled all around us, and we were

enveloped in a fine, clammy drizzle. I wondered whether Mrs Fosdyke's pampered pets were used to the rigours of life in the open air. I felt very chilly myself.

Then I heard Armand shout again. It sounded like, "Are you hungry?"

"Yes, are you?"

"Starving," came the reply.

Our conversation seemed like the signal for an orchestra of frogs, whose melodious croaking filled the air. Their lullaby must have sent me off to sleep.

During the night I awakened. My left leg felt completely numb. I could move it only with the greatest difficulty. The night was hushed and secretly still, the sound of falling raindrops magnified unnaturally by the silence. Even the frogs' orchestra had ended its performance.

I was obsessed by the conviction that Armand was no longer under his tree. He had either wandered off in the forest and not been able to find his way back, or been dragged off to be devoured by a predator. In my half-asleep state I felt illogically cross with Armand. Maybe he had even captured his monkey and was now sleeping soundly in the warm, dry bed at the hotel. I shouted hoarsely, "Armand!" but there was no answer. I was deserted. I slept again, convinced that I was alone in the forest.

But when I was awakened again it was through Armand shaking my shoulder, and it was already dawn. I blinked up at him as he said, "How long have you had that monkey on your lap?"

"Monkey, what monkey?" I asked, still in a daze. Then I remembered, and looking down, saw two small arms encircling my waist, the little head resting on my arm. The expression on that sleeping monkey's face was one of saintly innocence.

"Good heavens!" I said, struggling to my feet with Armand's help. "Where's yours?" I tried not to wake the sleeper.

"It's already in its box," Armand replied. "Some Africans came along just before dawn and wondered what on earth a white man was doing fast asleep on the ground under a tree. When I told them, they climbed up and chased it down and I caught it."

We walked back to the jeep stiffly, and this time had no trouble in shutting the two sleepy creatures in together.

We had a large and welcome breakfast at the hotel: eggs and bacon and plenty of good hot coffee. After a bath and change of clothes we felt less bedraggled and went to feed the monkeys before the last lap of our eventful journey.

For the first time we blessed Mrs Fosdyke. She had had a small door cut into the side of the monkeys' box and we were able to put bananas and water in for our guests without fear of a further escape. They seemed very subdued and we reached Entebbe without further incident.

As we slowed down at the airfield, Armand said, voicing our common fear, "I only hope the Glossops are here to meet us."

I looked around. "Yes, there they are," I said with relief. I pointed to a man dressed in white shorts and shirt, and a woman in a flower-printed sun-dress. They were both thin and middle-aged and peered anxiously about, as if waiting for someone. I felt sure these were the Glossops. I was right. We were evidently expected —Mrs Fosdyke must have telegraphed. They waved and came over.

At once Mrs Glossop said, with a worried look, without greeting us, "Are they safe? Are Mrs Fosdyke's pets safe? Where are they?"

"They're in the back," said Armand. "And we are *all* perfectly safe, thank you."

"I do hope they haven't suffered from the journey, jolting about in the back, poor little things. Look at them, Joe, don't they look pathetic?"

As Joe peered into the back of the jeep, a young man's voice broke in on us.

"Sorry to hurry you, Mr and Mrs Denis, but you'd better weigh in your luggage straight away. You haven't much time."

We unloaded the box first and thrust it at the Glossops. They stood by it protectively, making soothing noises. Then the monkey which had bitten Armand sneezed into Mrs Glossop's face.

At once she turned on me, and then shot an accusing look at Armand. "Oh," she said in a shocked voice. "They've caught cold!"

I could bear no more. Hastily jumping back into the jeep, I called to Armand. "Come on, we still have to leave the jeep at the garage," and we drove off.

At last, after a jumble of feverish activities, we were settled in our seats on the plane. I had never in my life been so grateful to know that in a few moments we would be airborne.

"Are you looking forward to Arabia, Michaela?" Armand asked. But I was staring out of the window. In the distance two figures could be seen, slowly carrying a large box to a truck. As the plane started to taxi, I could have sworn that one of them gave a sudden cry, and held up a hand.

I turned back to Armand, giggling. "Arabia, darling? Oh, anywhere will be heaven."

223

Armand looked at me strangely. The plane rose and Africa was below us: majestic, turbulent Africa. Mrs Fosdyke, the Glossops, even the little darlings, were lost, obliterated in the blue distance. I sank back with a sigh and took Armand's hand.

Arabia, Asia, the East. All this lay ahead, a great deal of hard work, too; but we were very lucky, I thought, to see so much of the beautiful world. And yet could anything replace Africa for me? Somewhere far below us was Nairobi, and near it, our house. The thought was comforting. However far we might travel, this would some day be our home.